AMERICA WITHOUT VIOLENCE

AMERICA
WITHOUT
VIOLENCE

*Why Violence Persists
And How You Can Stop It*

Michael N. Nagler

ISLAND PRESS
Covelo, California

This book was written as a project of the Marin Educational Training and Advisory Center.

The author gratefully acknowledges permission granted by the following organizations and individuals to reproduce material from their works: Bobbs-Merrill Company for excerpts from *Nonviolence in America*, copyright © 1966 by Staughton Lynd; Robert E. L. Farmer; Frank Zappa Music, Inc. for lyrics from the song "I'm the Slime"; Navajivan Trust for Gandhi quotes from various publications; *San Francisco Chronicle* for excerpt from column by Charles McCabe, copyright © 1980 by San Francisco Chronicle; Simon & Schuster for excerpt from *The Giants,* copyright © 1977 by Richard J. Barnet. See "References and Notes" for specific citations.

Library of Congress Cataloging in Publication Data

Nagler, Michael N.
    America without violence.

    Bibliography: p.
    Includes index.
    1. Violence—United States. 2. Nonviolence.
I. Title.
HN90.V5N33   303.6'0973   82-7180
ISBN 0-933280-13-0   AACR2
ISBN 0-933280-14-9 (pbk.)

Editor: *Judy Chaffin*
Text design: *Diana Fairbanks*
Cover and jacket design: *Howard Jacobsen*
Graphs: *Ed Robertson*
Production supervision and coordination: *Linda Gunnarson*
Typeset in Garamond (Old Style) by *Dharma Press* of Oakland, California; printed and bound by *BookCrafters* in Fredericksburg, Virginia

CONTENTS

FOREWORD

My willingness to introduce this interesting and important book by Professor Michael N. Nagler was stimulated by learning of the experience that had galvanized his own motivation. This was the murder of Lucille, "an ideal student," on the Berkeley campus of the University of California in the spring of 1976. Recalling that tragedy brought flooding back to me memories of our attempt to develop research on violence here at the University of California, Los Angeles, and the dreadful circumstance that precipitated our ambitious attempt to tackle the problem.

When I came to UCLA in 1969, a top priority was to organize the world's first comprehensive, multidisciplinary center for research on life-threatening behavior. Research programs on *collective* violence—war, racial and religious strife, tribal and ethnic conflict, urban riots, etc.—while few, at least had been initiated elsewhere. But the scientific study of *personal* violence—involving one or two people, or within groups as small as a family—was sporadic at best, and no major university had undertaken such work despite the steady rise in violent crime in America during the 1960s.

At UCLA, I discussed with colleagues, and progressively revised, a general strategy for research on violence that I had worked out previously during a 1966–67 sabbatical as a Fellow at the Center for Advanced Study in the Behavioral Sciences at Stanford. However, local resources were not sufficient to initiate such a complex and expensive venture, and outside support for our work proved difficult to obtain. Months went by with little accomplished other than discussions about future research and a series of colloquia on violence featuring distinguished guest speakers in the field.

Then, in the early evening of December 15, 1970, while resisting a rape attempt in a UCLA parking structure, Sunny Lynn Dagowitz was murdered.

All of Professor Nagler's words about Lucille apply to Sunny: bright, responsive, a beautiful person, affectionate, idealistic, sincere.

She had been working late as a volunteer in a project to help underprivileged students. She was the only child of devoted parents who were themselves almost destroyed by their devastating loss.

In the aftermath of this tragedy, a shocked faculty determined that our hopes for a research program on violence must be carried forward without delay. Nevertheless, the planning process was careful and prolonged, and in the fall of 1972 we finally approached the California State Department of Health with a preliminary proposal for a large grant, followed by a more fully developed protocol the next spring.

After several months of negotiations, the Department of Health agreed to support the UCLA proposal, and asked the California Council on Criminal Justice to put up half the money from its federal funds. Following extensive hearings, the Council unanimously endorsed the UCLA program, and funding for the first three years of the new center's work appeared to be assured.

The University's program was multidisciplinary and would provide an integrated consideration of how medical, psychological, social, and cultural factors interact to influence the act of violence, its perpetrator, and its victim. While biological variables were included in several studies, primary emphasis was on the psychological and sociocultural aspects of certain types of life-threatening behavior. Collective violence was excluded; the focus was to be on the individual and the small group, including the family.

Unfortunately, because of a complex set of circumstances, the state legislature blocked funds for our project. Rumors had been circulated that dangerous experimentation, such as psychosurgery, was to be carried out—rumors that came to be accepted by well-meaning community members, who, to our dismay, rarely checked with the University to learn the facts. The outcome was the abandonment of a program that not only would have studied violence within an academic setting, but would have had practical application in the community, including crisis centers to assist those seeking help in controlling violent impulses, treatment for perpetrators and victims, and support for the survivors of those who die violently.

I cite this only to show, as Professor Nagler does in another way in Chapter 3, the extent to which many people, seemingly opposed to violence, nevertheless have unconsciously associated violence with freedom, and believe that to control the one means losing the other.

Nevertheless, despite the loss of our multidisciplinary center for studying violence, individual investigators, including myself, have continued to pursue the development of new knowledge in this field. My own work has concentrated on the extent to which perpetrators of the most egregious violence often prove to have been themselves victims of violence in childhood. Prevention of child abuse and neglect is, in my view, of critical importance if the epidemic of violence now afflicting the United States is ever to be controlled.

Yes, "epidemic" is the correct term. In the past twenty years the annual rate of violent crime has risen from 161 to 581 per 100,000 population in the United States. In two decades the homicide rate has more than doubled; in Los Angeles it has increased more than fourfold. Since 1960 rape has increased fourfold nationwide, armed robbery the same. If the morbidity and mortality rates represented by such a staggering rise in violence had been due to any other cause—a microbe, for example—it would long since have been termed an epidemic. Centers for disease control, and billions in public and private funds, would have been poured into research to bring the plague to an end. Inexplicably, however, in the case of death and disaster resulting from attacks by people on themselves or on each other, we have made no special effort to add new knowledge essential to halt the epidemic.

There are many important approaches to the problem of interpersonal violence that remain to be explored. For example, more than half of all violent deaths in America (including murder, suicide, and fatal accidents) are alcohol-related. Most important of all, however, is that we must stop taking violence for granted, adapting to it, accepting it, shrugging off attempts to change things, and ignoring those who cry out against it.

The author of this book cries out against violence in a way that cannot be ignored. His fresh and clear-eyed view of the violence problem provides a splendid example of what this field needs today: originality, creativity, new and fearless approaches. If there is any hope for us humans to build an America—and then a world—without violence, it will be because personal strategies, like Professor Nagler's, ultimately involve a sufficient number of people. Then perhaps the humane strategy of such enlightened individuals will merge with a humane public policy, and violence shall finally diminish in our suffering land.

LOUIS JOLYON WEST, M.D.
Director, Neuropsychiatric Institute, and
Chairman, Department of Psychiatry and
Biobehavioral Sciences, UCLA School of Medicine

DEDICATORY PREFACE

In the spring of 1976 I was team-teaching a beginning religion course on the Berkeley campus, and it was then that I met Lucille. She was extremely bright, instinctively responded to the best my partner and I came up with: an ideal student. Besides, she was a beautiful person—affectionate, sincere, attractive, somehow taking the right things in life seriously but with great reserves of humor. Almost at once, Carol and I grew terribly fond of her.

But tragedy lay in wait for Lucille, a modern tragedy some version of which all of us have come to fear. A man attacked her as she tried to cross a wooded area to leave campus after her last class. Lucille wasn't one to yield. By the time someone went for a policeman she was badly beaten and lay deep in a coma.

I suppose none of us who knew her ever believed she wouldn't make it. Lucille had so much to live for—happily married, serious interests in life, talented, every possibility ahead of her. We waited for the phone call every day that she lay in the hospital; for Fred, her husband, knew how much we cared about her, and he was with her every day, searching the invisible for some way to bring recognition back to her injured body. It was my daughter who took the last phone call and burst into our room saying, "Daddy, Lucille is dead."

For some days, the campus was in a kind of shock. A beautiful coed, just about to graduate with a degree in art, killed during an attempted rape. But for us the shock was deeper. There are some things that all of us seem to make our peace with, but then a tragedy strikes too close and you no longer can. Some wounds don't heal. We felt that we had aged ten years in eleven days.

And so, while the campus gradually returned to normal, I did not. I found myself thinking about things that had happened before Lucille was killed that seemed normal at the time. For example, I thought about a lecture I had heard by a prominent criminologist who happened to speak about the growing number of molestations of women in the campus area: It wasn't so much that he said his profession had no light to shed on the subject—though that could be alarming enough—but that he declared that *nobody* could say anything about it, such things were "impossible" to comprehend. It reminded me of a humanities colleague who had written, "Neither primitive nor modern man has yet succeeded in identifying the microbe responsible for the dread disease of violence," and of a well-known psychiatrist who echoed, "We really don't know what causes crime." And in thinking back over all these things, something in me rebelled. I could not, and I cannot, accept that we have all been dumped here on this planet with no way to shape our own society or exert a modest control on our own destiny. I reject the notion that the destiny of the human experiment is to end without meaning in a nuclear "exchange" or at the end of a mugger's handgun.

I decided to postpone other things and to find out for myself what causes violence and what to do about it. This book is the result of that decision. You will see, I think, that the search has not been fruitless. But the further I got, the more sympathy I had with those experts who are fighting shy of telling us the answer: There is no cause of violence other than ourselves. The way, or ways, to cure this scourge, then, are not particularly obscure, but neither are they always pleasant. Yet I feel sure that some will see the implications of what I have written and carry them further in their own thinking and in their own lives. If so, we may be able to say without triteness that although Lucille should not have died, perhaps she has not died entirely in vain.

Berkeley, California
February 1982

ACKNOWLEDGMENTS

If the tale were told, the list of people who helped one way or other with the creation of this book would be longer than most readers could be expected to peruse. I would be left responsible only for some of its defects, in fact. Let me therefore thank here only a selected list: Olivia Moore, Barbara Elsasser, Lark Turner, Jan Mattlock, and Rita Maran, who typed the rangy manuscript, the latter two also giving criticism when needed and encouragement when there was an opening. Quite a few of my academic colleagues—Ashley Montagu, Sherwood Washburn, Gerald Berreman, James Larson, Diana Baumrind, John Gofman, Alberta Siegel among them—were generous with their expertise. I cannot adequately thank Norman Cousins for his precious time and encouragement. My ideas for the book had been worked out on three successive generations of students in my nonviolence course at UC, Berkeley—I thank them too. Terry Morrison and Nick Harvey, good friend and master of editorial midwifery, brought out of me what I really meant before I knew I meant it, giving the manuscript its shape and making Judy Chaffin's job more civilized by the time it reached her editorial desk, for the moment at Island Press. (At Island Press, the author is adopted along with the book; it has been a joy to work with them.) Thanks are due to Jerry Mander for much help—and a title. Dorothy Nagler, not content with giving the author birth, helped him check some references at the end. As with most causes of this kind, there were superb volunteers—Peter Brown, Paula Terrey, Bev Holmes, Steve Lightman, to name a few—who helped for neither favor nor remuneration but because they want a world without violence. My wife and children put up with what authors' families must perennially endure. My teacher, Eknath Easwaran, gave me the inspiration to attempt this book, and the courage. He has guided me for more than a decade to whatever wisdom I possess.

Part One

THE PROBLEM
AND ITS CAUSES

1 | The Lie of Otherness

There are some subjects about which you will learn the truth more accurately from the first man you meet in the street than from people who have made a lifelong and accurate study of it.

George Bernard Shaw

It is very difficult to think clearly about violence. Having pondered and discussed the subject for many years, I know that heat, not light, is the form of energy it immediately produces. In a sense, we would not want it any other way. If the problem of violence did not arouse strong feelings in us, I am not sure we would consider ourselves fully human. What is more, where would we find the motivation to confront it?

By themselves, however, strong emotional reactions are not always helpful. Fear, confusion, anger, bitterness, frustration—all of which are common responses to violence today—can cloud the mind and make people do things that actually cause the problem to worsen. So can the feeling of helplessness, or paralysis, which makes people do nothing at all about the problem that is slowly making our age such an unhappy one to live in. Many try not to think about violence. It's someone else's problem; the police will handle it—or the Defense Department. Or no one will: You can't change human nature. There are experts to buttress these reactions, such as the retired British major general who wrote *Living with Terrorism*, and whose message is just that—learn to live with it. But the police can't handle the problem, as we shall see, nor can the Department of Defense. And how are we supposed to "live with" these incidents of terrorism, which seem to be getting more frequent by a rate of about 20 percent a year? Experts or no experts, these appeals to fatalism have got to be strenuously rejected. As sociologist Knud Larsen put it, "Appeals to instinctive or generic explanations of violence doom mankind to a perpetual state of hostility. Anyone vaguely familiar with

3

psychology can recognize that in this conception lie the roots of the self-fulfilling prophecy."

Somewhere between overreacting and not reacting lies the very common response of doing something about the *symptoms*. Recently a cab driver in Santa Rosa, California, was assaulted by one of her fares. The general tone of advice she was given was, "Never pick up a guy at the Greyhound station again."

One could fill volumes with what this reaction leaves out of account. I don't mean only the fact that disturbed men do not restrict their operations to Greyhound stations: There is the fact that violent attacks on women are increasing all over the country (by 116 percent between 1960 and 1969), the fact that relationships between men and women in general are becoming more vexed, the fact that sexual inhibitions are dissolving, the fact that violence of every kind is getting worse in most areas of the world. But the most important thing to note in the very common reaction of people to this episode is the assumption that violence itself cannot be confronted. *X* amount of violence is inevitable. Only certain forms of it—certain delivery points, as it were—can be avoided.

In progressive planning circles today this is called a "downstream solution"—it involves looking for a way to fish bodies out of the river, but never a thought of going upstream to repair the bridge. Most of the responses we are making to violence today are downstream solutions: Stiffer jail sentences, lighter jail sentences, carrying guns, locking your doors and windows, threatening hostile powers with massive reprisals —all these are attempts to baffle particular forms of violence or retaliate after they have happened. None of them tries to confront the *causes* of violence, to do anything about violence itself.

> In trying to solve the terrifying problems that face us in the world today, we naturally turn to the things we do best. We play from strength, and our strength is science and technology. To contain a population explosion we look for better methods of birth control. Threatened by a nuclear holocaust, we build bigger deterrent forces and antiballistic missile systems. But things get steadily worse, and it is disheartening to find that technology itself is increasingly at fault.

This observation by the well-known psychologist B. F. Skinner describes our dilemma perfectly. Notice how often we turn to *things* to solve a problem of violence: chemical Mace for women who have to walk about alone; guns for schoolteachers, store owners, householders, park rangers; missiles for members of NATO. But a problem of violence can never be solved by things, because it doesn't arise from things. It arises from people. Violence—all violence—is a disorder of human relationships. Think of whatever form of the problem you wish— muggings, homicide, rape, or war. Is it a thing, or is it a bad human relationship in a time when all human relationships are going bad?

HOW NOT TO BE SECURE

Truth can be that simple, though it is not always easy to make the truth one's own and put it to its proper use. The truism that violence is caused by people has even been used to *prevent* a very sensible way of controlling violence: "Guns don't kill people; only people kill people" (so let's not control guns). If we take this very reaction and explore the ideas and misconceptions that lie behind it, we may come to a better understanding of the problem of gun control. We may also discover just what it is in human relationships that is going wrong. What is the besetting disorder that produces violence?

Everyone knows that keeping a handgun can be dangerous (though not precisely how dangerous: From as early as 1966, about 2,500 adults and children have been accidentally shot to death with them every year). Why do people keep them nonetheless? The answer was never put more simply than it was by Gordon Liddy, the future Watergate "plumber," writing in the National Rifle Association organ, *Guns and Ammo*: "There is a profound sense of security felt by some 45 million firearms-owning citizens in the knowledge that they have in their homes a gun." It is not only gun lobbyists and cranks who share this sentiment. Forty-five million handguns (now over fifty million) makes one weapon for every fourth man, woman, and child in the nation, one in every other home—all to make those people and those homes secure.

Unfortunately, they have no such effect. Statistics show that if you keep a gun in your home it is *five times* more likely to harm someone in your own family than an intruder. People who keep guns are twice as likely to meet with murder or accidental death or injury or suicide than those who do not.

There have been a fair number of riots in the United States, about 500 from 1953 to 1970. After one of the worst, which took place in the "hot summer" of 1967 in Detroit and cost the lives of forty people, Detroit homeowners "brought into their homes and lives an unprecedented arsenal of handguns for self-defense." By some accounts the number of guns in the city doubled, to 500,000. This was an irrational reaction since the rioting had vented itself not against homes but against businesses and most of these within the black community. But it was not without effect: The homicide rate in the city also doubled.

In a three-year study carried out in rural Ohio it was discovered that although over half the families in the 900 homes being studied kept guns and locked their doors at night, it made *no difference whatever* in the amount of burglary and vandalism they suffered. And, ironically, one of the items housebreakers most consistently go for is the household gun; more than 100,000 such weapons fall into the hands of intruders every year.

What props up the illusion that handguns give security in the face of the dismal facts about what they actually do? To answer that most householders don't know these facts will not do. The facts are accessible; we are really seeking to understand why most of us do not know them. Let's look at the following example. In 1979, the local papers reported that a woman who lived alone in Oakland, California, successfully defended herself with her revolver against two black assailants who entered her home during the night. They had come expressly to kill her. She shot one of them, said the paper, and the other took to his heels. Ironically, the paper pointed out, they had had the wrong woman all along. They were after another woman who lived alone on the same block and who was a potential witness in an ongoing murder trial.

But it wasn't only the would-be assassins who were confused. Several days later the newspaper printed a hardly noticeable retraction near the back pages, which explained that although the woman who was mistakenly attacked did indeed have a gun, she had never fired it. Her assailant was somehow killed by his own partner. People see what they pay attention to and believe what they are prepared to understand. The image of a householder using a potent weapon to defend the home against malevolent intruders is rooted in ancient myths about chaos and order. These myths predispose us to see only the "facts" that fit them, a process that is very much aggravated by modern mass media. Facts that don't fit into our imagery, even if closer to the truth, are relegated to the back pages.

The sense of security that comes from having a gun is not "profound," as Mr. Liddy would have us believe, but false. Guns make life more dangerous, not less. About two-thirds of the handgun deaths that are now occurring are not premeditated. They are not felony-related crimes but take place between friends or spouses or lovers (especially jealous spouses or lovers) who would have acted much less intemperately, or at least with much less fatal effect, if a handgun had not been around. There is another reason that handguns make life risky. Even less well known and even more revealing is the fact that about a third of all homicides fall into a category that criminologists call "victim precipitated." Someone who rightly or wrongly thinks he is about to be attacked pulls out a weapon "for defense" and is promptly slain. The soon-to-be victim's knife or gun precipitates the very event that is feared. The dynamics of this effect are so predictable that some criminologists think many such deaths are actually a kind of suicide by proxy. Be that as it may, the following words of an experienced felon confirm what criminologists are saying about victim-precipitated shootings:

> Firearms in the hands of private citizens are dangerous. Almost all handguns used by me and others in my line of work were obtained by taking them away from people who were scared stiff and didn't know how to use them. I never bought a gun in my life.... Sometimes they get panicky and shoot a hole in the wall—or their own foot. The intruder is then forced to fire a shot that is far better aimed.
>
> I have to laugh when I hear the pro-gun people say, "If you ban guns only the criminals will have them." The truth is, if guns were banned there would be fewer guns in the hands of all of us, and that would mean fewer criminals and fewer gunshot wounds and fatalities.

Clearly our gut reactions about how to protect ourselves can be off the mark. The Quakers like to relate that during the terrible Irish wars of 1688–91, no Irish Quaker, with one exception, was injured. Though technically Protestant, the Quakers refused to take sides in the conflict and kept their homes and hearts open to Catholic and Protestant alike, whoever needed medical attention or refuge from the disaster. There were severe threats from both sides against the unarmed Quakers, but somehow those threats were never carried out. However, one young man lost his nerve. He strapped on his sword and uniform and ran to the nearby garrison for protection. He never made it.

WHEN IS A MODEL NOT A MODEL?

Besides being an attempt to solve the problem of violence by using things, the use of guns for protection reflects a general theory about human behavior. The guns don't even have to be fired, some people say; just knowing that they are there makes you feel safer; just knowing that they are there makes a potential aggressor think twice about attacking. This is the famous theory of deterrence. It forms a part of our national policy toward the Soviet Union—and of theirs toward us. It forms no small part of our theory of criminal justice and other approaches to violence, too.

Do weaponry, and the fear of reprisal, and other aspects of the deterrent strategy work? Certainly many people think so. One of the first things Senator Strom Thurmond said about his new role as chairman of the important Senate Judiciary Committee was that he would work to bring back the death penalty because it deters crime and we have so much of it to deter.

Does the death penalty deter crime? Homicide is the crime for which one stands the greatest risk of being apprehended and faces the severest penalties; yet it is the fastest-growing form of violent crime in the United States. "There is no significant correlation," says Dr. Donald Lunde, a Stanford professor of psychiatry and authority on legal insanity, "either positive or negative, between the threat of the death penalty and the homicide rate. Few murderers consider beforehand what they will do or what might befall them after their crime." Indeed, according to a thorough statistical analysis carried out by Professors W. J. Bowers and G. L. Pierce of the Center for Applied Social Research at Northeastern University, the death penalty slightly *increases* the rate of homicide.

The theory of deterrence works when an adversary is entirely rational and can weigh the pros and cons of what will happen after he or she attacks—which, as we have just heard from Dr. Lunde, is rarely the case, at least for the most prevalent form of homicide. But for other forms of criminal behavior, too, rationality is conspicuous by its absence. Two of the most successful criminal rehabilitators of recent years, S. E. Samenow and the late Dr. S. Yochelson, have shown that one of the strongest motivating factors for crime is excitement, so that a certain amount of risk may not deter the person contemplating a crime, but actually be provocative. Psychiatrist Eric Berne, author of *Games People Play*, argued that for not a few people whom we call criminals crime and punishment form part of an unconscious pattern that drives them compulsively, so that the more certain the punishment is, the more likely it is to stimulate the crime.

Clearly, the notion that we can protect our homes by making the potential intruders' fear of reprisal greater than their desire for our silverware is far too simplistic. Human motivation is much more than a one-dimensional cost-benefit analysis. Guns and fists and prison bars seem compelling in their simplicity, but they compel *us* to misunderstand human relationships.

In the phenomenon of victim-precipitated homicide (or suicide), the worst drawback of deterrence is not that it misjudges relationships but that it *changes* them. By assuming that we are going to be attacked, by preparing to retaliate, we worsen the relationship between ourselves and potential attackers—who, after all, are also potential nonattackers. Without referring to the criminal's need for excitement or for punishment, Bowers and Pierce were able to suggest how the death penalty could stimulate some homicides: by "brutalizing" the relationships among people—cheapening the value of life in general and causing a further erosion in the natural sympathy people have for one another. From this standpoint, death imposed by the state is not very different from death inflicted by an individual. If we want compelling simplicity, the slogan of those who protest the death penalty has much to recommend it: "Why do we kill people who kill people to show that killing people is wrong?"

Similarly, in the relationships of nations, as Robert C. Johansen, President of the Institute for World Order, has pointed out: "By its reliance on military strength for much of its diplomacy . . . the United States [the same could be said of the Soviet Union] does far more to legitimize the role of military power than to delegitimize it." Where power is legitimized, other modes of relationship like compassion and mutual responsibility are compromised. It is important to realize, however, that people who have conservative ideologies are not the only ones who consider deterrence, retaliation, and the like, legitimate. A student of mine who was pursuing a doctorate in theology once explained to me and the other members of his examination committee that he was very "dovish" and opposed to the ongoing war in South Vietnam. But when it came to what he thought should be done about the war, he advocated what he called "controlled violence": You do bomb the local draft board to discourage further escalations of the war, but you make sure that everyone is out of the building first. I could have pointed out to him that the U.S. Army was practicing "controlled violence" at that moment in Vietnam, under names like "surgical military operations." But I was too depressed.

That people of so many different persuasions, some of little special education and some who are accounted experts, are all coming up with repetitively wrong solutions to a fundamental problem like violence, points to an underlying dilemma: We have a fundamentally wrong model of human relationships.

None of us can understand the world around us without some kind of model—some would call it a paradigm or a root metaphor—of how that world works. Cultures, also, develop collective models that represent in appropriately simplified terms the psychodynamic processes and forces underlying all interactions of human beings with one another and their environment. These models make it possible for members of common cultures to coexist and to cooperate; and the absence of a mutually intelligible model between different cultures has accounted for not a little of the friction and hostility between them.

There is therefore no question of trying to function either as an individual or as a culture without such a model. There is definitely a question, however, of how long a particular model continues to be adequate. The rapidly changing conditions of modern life, the bigness of society, the pace of living, the interaccessibility of peoples and states to one another, and advances in the technology of weapons, have brought with them the need for an expanded model, an advancement in understanding, that we have not yet filled. "The splitting of the atom," said Einstein, "has changed everything, save our mode of thinking, and thus we drift towards unparalleled catastrophe."

Simply put, the working model we have brought with us from the past is that for all intents and purposes human beings are precisely what they seem: separate packages of physical and mental life, cut off from one another by the very laws of time and space. In this book I propose another model, though hardly one that has never been proposed before: that despite these appearances the entire human community, and indeed the entire web of life in which that community is sustained, is but one system—a kind of vast, multipartite organism.

With regard to violence, you will see at once how radically these two models differ. By the prevailing model I can hurt you without hurting myself, and therefore violence can be a legitimate way of influencing you or getting what I want. If you frustrate me, or if you in some way injure me, naturally I might be inclined to hurt you back. But by the new model all this is quite impossible. The hand cannot punish the stomach because there is some disagreement about eating.

Einstein himself gave the best definition of this new model that I know of, in a letter of condolence to a rabbi whose wife could not be consoled over the death of their daughter. The passage reads:

> A human being is a part of the whole, called by us the "universe," a part limited in time and space. He experiences himself, his thoughts and feelings, as something separated from the rest—a kind of optical delusion of his consciousness. This delusion is a kind of prison for us, restricting us to our personal desires and to affection for a few persons nearest to us. Our task must be to free ourselves from this prison by widening our circle of compassion to embrace all living creatures and the whole of nature in its beauty.

We are one; we appear separate; our task must be to cross from that appearance of separateness to that reality of oneness by constantly "widening our circle of compassion."

For our purposes, it is not important to decide whether this great vision of the unity of life is "true." Fascinating as it would be to speculate on that profound question, we need not wait for philosophers to give us a definitive answer, assuming there were such an answer. The point is that as a *working model* the hypothesis that all life is one is infinitely superior to the old hypothesis of separateness.

How much longer can we sustain the ethic that permits any factory to dump its refuse into the nearby river or any nation to help itself to the resources of a weaker or less developed nation? Don't we all have to breathe the same air and drink the same water; don't we all suffer when the global economic system is damaged? If the past two decades have taught us anything, it is that the entire planet is a single, interrelated system, an ecosystem (which means a single home for all of us), and we must learn to respect and live by that model to survive.

That the model works can be tested in our own everyday experiences, if we only have the frame of reference to understand them. I once overheard a conversation between two young women who were trading notes about the difficulties of life with their respective boyfriends. One of them finally said, "I don't know why things go better when I'm *nice* to the creep; they just do." She was seeing the unity of life at work, without having a name for it or a conscious model with which to understand it. And the model can work with crime and violence, as in the long run deterrence does *not*. The new model tells us why: When you strip away the euphemism, "deterrence" is just newspeak for plain old threatening. To threaten people is to treat them as very "other." Our national "credible retaliatory posture" is not essentially an advance over the posture of a chimpanzee brandishing a stick.

In contrast, what the Irish Quakers practiced *did* work, and though there is no way of understanding this by the old model of separateness, it makes perfect sense by a model that acknowledges the intimate relationship of all human communities. By such a model, the Quaker ethos of respecting "that of God in every man," and therefore of refraining from regarding any person or group as somehow inferior to or, in the last analysis, really other than one's own, would obviously work, because it corresponds to reality.

In practical terms, then, what should we watch out for if we want to try to put this new model to use? Here let's enlist an observation made by two well-respected authorities on different and apparently unrelated forms of violence.

The first is Dr. Donald Lunde. In comparing a type of sadistic homicide with the collective injustices sometimes perpetrated by political states—the one a recognized crime, the other by some standards within the law—he finds that in both cases the perpetrators of these acts dehumanize their intended victims and look on them not as people but as inanimate objects. To the murderers, "the victims may be viewed as 'life-sized dolls' rather than as fellow human beings," while in collective, political violence, "the victims may be perceived as 'enemies of the state' . . . or some kind of faceless inhuman objects."

Professor Kenneth Boulding, the distinguished economist and

worldwide authority on war and peace, is the second. "Alienation," writes Professor Boulding, "is an important source of violence." He continues:

> International war is only possible because the enemy is defined as a foreigner and not as a member of the society.... In internal war, likewise, alienation is of great importance. The Irish Republican Army people who plant bombs which kill the innocent could only do so if they were deeply alienated not only from their own society but in a sense from all society. *If they ever thought of their victims as real people,* one doubts whether they could bring themselves to these acts. Fortunately, in most human beings, alienation rarely rises to this level.

What those authorities are calling alienation and dehumanization is increasing on every hand today, and so is violence. Whether that violence is murder or persecution or terrorism or war, it is carried out by human beings who regard one another as alien to themselves, thus violating the natural spirit of cooperation and the unity that could prevail among them. The very word "violence" implies as much, being closely akin to "violate." Every act of violence implies and enacts a violation or, as psychiatrist Robert Jay Lifton put it, a "wound in the order of being." The dissolution of that order, the tearing of that seamless web—alienation, in a word—is the essential disorder of relationships that is the chief cause of violence.

In practical terms, then, we can examine any solution proposed to a problem of violence according to the question, Does this help to decrease alienation? If it does not, the "solution" may be serviceable as a temporary stopgap, but it is no solution. If it actually increases alienation, as many contemporary measures do, the remedy is only going, in the long run, to exacerbate the malady.

This simple criterion enables us to push through a lot of confusion and tell what is really usable and what is not in the grab bag of incoherent, chaotic responses, public and private, learned and amateur, to the frightening increase of violence that is part of the modern condition. For example, late in 1980 many newspapers carried a report of the rise in crime across the nation for the preceding year: 12.1 million reported crimes (or one every three seconds, and this may be only half the crimes that actually occur); a 9 percent increase in reported crime of all kinds over 1978, and for violent crimes 11 percent. It was enough, pointed out the *San Francisco Chronicle*, to mean that one of every four Americans will be beaten, robbed, or raped every ten years if the trend goes unchecked. And how can we check it? An expert from the Stanford Research Institute gave us the following choices: "a combination of draconian police measures and sophisticated behavior modification techniques in prisons, including drugs and psychosurgery"; or "more sophisticated crime prevention methods, along with a shift in the social fabric to bring about a recovery of the family and the restoration of the educational system."

The first set of choices is really just a combination of ways to alienate further a set of people who are already badly alienated—those whom we like to brand as criminals. It hardly matters whether the procedures are "draconian" or "sophisticated"; indeed, the sophisticated set, including drugs and psychosurgery, about which we will have more to say in a later chapter, is the most barbaric. Drugs and surgery presuppose the greatest gulf between human beings, setting at nothing the possibility of appeal by reason or persuasion, inflicting the most insulting forms of manipulation on those held to be offensive.

The second set is an odd mixture. What most people mean by "crime prevention" today entails yet more alienation; the system recently set up in California by which anyone can phone in anonymous tips on whomever he or she thinks is up to no good is a typical example. But the other half suggests a real solution: a "shift in the social fabric."

The only real way to reduce crime and violence is by reducing the alienation that causes them. The model of unity can be applied in real-life situations by shifting values from competition to cooperation, from vindictiveness to compassion, and in other ways such as recovering family life and giving meaning to education, which the article identifies without furnishing practical suggestions. All these will be explored in the next chapters. Throughout this book the new model of unity will be implicitly or explicitly the guiding frame of reference.

Using the unity model as a thought experiment, as we have just done, can help us immediately to clarify what causes a particular form of violence and what should be done to cure it. But to actually implement that cure, we need more than a thought experiment. We need to assimilate this outlook into our systems so that it starts to permeate our behavior. Back when the public first became aware of the global food crisis, a distinguished demographer from my university, adopting an old military procedure for emergencies when the wounded were too numerous to rescue, proposed that the "have" nations concentrate on saving a few groups, those who are most like ourselves, and leave the rest—about one-third of the human race—to starve. The facts on which this exercise in "lifeboat ethics" were founded have been resoundingly refuted (there is more than enough food for everyone if it is distributed to those who need it), but my colleague's problem was not with the facts. His problem was in setting off on the wrong track by beginning all his thoughts about food scarcity, "since we all have to look out for ourselves." Excepting one or two public figures who asked to be among the first to starve, not wanting to live in the kind of world this professor envisioned, the monstrosity of his opening premise went unremarked. We must change to the degree that we—including experts like the demographer—begin instead with the premise, "since we are all in this together."

Here is another example of what is considered normal today, this one from one of the most morally concerned newspapers in the country:

> Should there be friendship in foreign affairs? Certainly not. Foreign policy is the conduct of the national interest. Whatever is done should be done not because someone once did a favor or kindness. . . . It should be done only if it furthers the national interest. . . . Shahs and Somozas never really serve any interest but their own. Washington should do the same.

Survival demands that we perceive the world clearly enough that we remember what happened to the shah and to Somoza and ask if we want that to happen to ourselves. It must become our first reaction not to ask, as the papers did during the Iranian hostage crisis in 1980, "What can the United States do to Iran?" (i.e., to hurt Iran) but to ask, *just as automatically*, "*Should* the United States do something to hurt Iran?" Is it wise? Is hurting our only alternative? Is there not a way we can seek reconciliation?

In other words, the way we perceive one another, the way we feel toward one another, and the way we behave toward one another must change. This is the task of which Einstein spoke, and it is truly the task of a lifetime. But the solution to violence now demands no less. Neither inertia nor lazy swatting at the problem with superficial, disorganized responses is affecting the root cause of violence. Mounting in every form, including the new spectre of annihilation by nuclear war, no force can stop it but that which could be released by digging new channels in our awareness of one another. "Fortunately," said Professor Boulding (about terrorism in Ireland), "in most human beings, alienation rarely rises to this level." Can we really afford to leave such things to chance?

Violence is a Hydra-headed monster. The Hydra of ancient myth had poisonous blood as well as those heads that would regenerate as Hercules tried to cut them off, one at a time. Alienation is our Hydra's poison. Unless we find a cure for that, and not just cast about for a sharper sword to cut at the monster's many heads, it will be a matter of time and chance as to which of those snarling manifestations bites us first.

2 | The Uses of Violence

*And about all the passions and desires and miseries and
pleasures in the mind which accompany our every action,
this is what imitative art produces: it waters what
should be allowed to dry up, and puts in charge of our
lives what we should rule over if we want to grow better
and happier instead of worse and more miserable.*

Plato
Republic 10.606d

*Nothing Orwell invented for 1984 is quite as horrifying
[as] what television has done to the soul of man. And
this was not done by some malevolent dictator. It was
done willingly by people who designate their own species as
sapient.*

Charles McCabe
San Francisco Chronicle

The idea that all life is one has been in the air for centuries. We
have seen already how easily it can explain why some of our approaches
to violence have not worked. But this model is far from popular. It
arouses disturbing reflections about how we construct our policies and
lead our lives. It makes us wonder how much society as we know it
depends on this inherently questionable power: Violence is the "bottom line" in society's efforts to control crime, and it informs all
negotiations in the uneasy relationships of states. But I want to focus
here on the newest and in many ways the strangest of all uses of
violence—violence as "entertainment." Eventually, *all* forms of violence
have to go. But for various reasons the violent obsession of our
media—as news, as "sports," or as fiction—is the place to start.

SELF-DECEPTION AND VIOLENCE

Newspapers have a way of framing headlines that can make us miss
the point of the stories that unfold beneath them. For example, in the

San Francisco Chronicle for August 27, 1978, there was a story headed "I Just Went Crazy." It was about a man who lost control of himself when he caught his daughters making marijuana cigarettes, and killed them. In a panic, the story said, the man went on to kill his wife when she came home, after which he fled to another city, where he remarried and assumed a new identity. Toward the end of the story (for those who read that far) was a fleeting reference to something seen by a neighbor in the curiously empty household: "Most significant to her was a collection of about thirty murder mysteries. One had passages underlined showing how to commit a murder, she testified."

If you believe it is impossible to understand how violence comes about (or do anything to prevent it), you might well believe that this man "just went crazy." But in reality he no more "just went" that way than a Nureyev "just" turns into a ballet star or a scientist "just" stumbles on a Nobel Prize. By learning to enjoy violence, then contemplating violence, the man in the story made himself more and more prone to violence. When the right (wrong) set of circumstances developed, it spilled out of him. Whether he knew what he was doing all along is another question. The question we have to ask is, How can it be a coincidence that the violence he kept dwelling on day by day eventually burst forth?

What is shocking is that almost all of us are flirting with violence in some degree. Most murder mysteries in fact present comparatively mild forms of it. But ever since Alfred Hitchcock released his classic thriller *Psycho* in the summer of 1960 and three young men committed murders in close imitation of the film (one of them murdering his own grandmother), we have been steadily sliding into the present era of "ultra-violence." As the detail and brutality of the violence presented slowly escalated—the technicolor, the slow motion, the heightened realism—we prepared ourselves for the phenomenon of the gang warfare film. When *Boulevard Nights* and *The Warriors* were released in 1979, members of the audience were so aroused that they started shooting in the theater. Eight people were killed at these films, five wounded, and the response was classic "downstream": The distributor provides a security guard at every showing, and non–gang members are advised to remain outside the line of fire during the performance. The mayor of San Francisco was loudly criticized merely for asking San Francisco theater managers not to show these films.

Violent films have helped to shape the direction of our national destiny, a role that lies disturbingly outside the democratic process. During World War II, President Roosevelt pointed with pride to the fact that America had never bombed civilian targets. But in 1944 he was persuaded to see a Walt Disney propaganda film called *Victory Through Air Power*, after which he allowed the military to do such bombings. (Many experts now think this move only stiffened waning Axis resistance.) President Nixon's decision to invade Cambodia seems likewise to have been prompted by his repeated viewings of the movie *Patton*.

Films seen in theaters are probably the second most influential medium through which acts of violence are encouraged or precipitated. Television is undoubtedly the first. In a survey of prison inmates, for example, reported by Nicholas Johnson, Chairman of the National Citizens Committee for Broadcasting, "ninety percent said they had improved their criminal talents by watching TV and forty percent had actually attempted crimes they first saw on TV."

And what about ordinary people, those of us who are neither prisoners nor presidents? Every available form of evidence suggests that our collective television diet of more than 500 killings every week is putting us through a veritable school for violence.

Consider these statistics:

☐ 96 percent of American homes have at least one television set.

☐ The average home has a set going 6 hours a day.

☐ In "ordinary" viewing, there are 8 violent episodes an hour.

☐ Between the ages of five and fifteen the average American child has watched the killing of 13,000 people. By age eighteen he or she will have logged more than 15,000 hours of this kind of exposure and taken in more than 20,000 acts of violence.

☐ By the time they are three, most children watch television at least 2 hours a day. Before they are old enough to go to school they are watching it for 6 to 7 hours a day, or *54 hours a week.*

☐ By the age of sixteen the average child spends as much time watching television as he or she does in school. By the time he or she gets to college, when the number of hours spent viewing begins to decline, the time spent watching television is equivalent to 5 years at an institution of higher learning.

☐ 97 percent of cartoons intended for children include acts of violence. By the criteria of the Media Action Research Center, an act of aggression occurs every 3½ minutes during children's Saturday morning programs. Dr. George Gerbner counts one every 2 minutes by similar criteria.

☐ In a typical recent year "children ... witnessed, on prime time television, 5,000 murders, rapes, beatings, and stabbings, 1,300 acts of adultery, and 2,700 sexually aggressive comments," according to a group of concerned mothers.

These figures give some idea of the "early window" through which modern children see life. If we identify television watching as "Cause," here are some statistics that we might label "Effects":

Murder: Murder is the fastest-growing cause of death in the United States. The average age of those who commit it has gone down 10 years (to age twenty-one) in a 10-year period; the youngest murderer now on record is three. The largest increase in deaths from homicide during this period occurred in the age group of children one to four. The likelihood of eventually being murdered in this country is escalating to one in twelve if present trends continue; in 1976 the rate climbed past one murder victim out of 10,000 Americans each year.

Other violent deaths: 5,182 young Americans were murdered in 1973 (for example), and 4,098 committed suicide (not counting the 3,000 traffic deaths, about one-sixth of the total, that are a form of suicide). The death rate these figures represent was 19 percent higher than in 1960–61, entirely due to deaths by violence, and the figure is steadily increasing.

Other acts of violence: According to FBI statistics, rapes and attempted rapes in schools increased 40.1 percent between 1970 and 1973. In February, 1979, students at Berkeley High School in Berkeley, California, reported twenty-nine violent incidents. After the arrest of four students and former students, the rate of robbery and assault returned to normal–"normal" being defined by a Berkeley police inspector as one assault or robbery *each week*. In 1979 nationwide, there were 12.1 million reported crimes, or one every three seconds.

These figures are not statistics to anyone who has lived through them. For the grandmother who watched her grandson shot to death in a restaurant by a man who wanted to try out his new handgun, or the parents who sit waiting for news of their missing children, or nearly anyone who lives in a modern city, such numbers do not even suggest the experiences behind them. My own children went to a high school far from a major city—but not beyond the reach of television. One of my son's classmates was addicted to violent programs, which he always mimicked parts of, carrying on "like a freshman," as my son said. One day this boy had an argument with my son and, shortly after, another argument with a friend in the gym. Before anyone knew what was happening he had pulled this friend out of the stands by the ankles, spun him around in midair, and slammed him down on the gymnasium floor. The victim escaped without serious injuries; but in a way none of us escaped injuries. My daughter came home sobbing that "it might have been Josh," and everyone involved began to regard everyone else a little bit more warily and suspiciously. Only a little of the human damage from violence is ever reported in the papers.

The direct connection between any particular act of violence and television viewing or exposure to other media violence is difficult to *prove*. Only in rare cases such as the *Psycho* murders, which occurred right after showings of the film at a time when murders of that kind were rare, and the fifteen suicides that were (as of 1981) linked to screenings of *The Deer Hunter* because they imitated the bizarre mode of killing it displayed, and the four people who were murdered "for the fun of it" in Indiana by a group of young people who had just seen *Helter-Skelter* can a particular act be traced, at least in part, to a particular media stimulus. However rare, one might think that these alone would be enough to start serious questioning of our right to watch as many violent images as we want. How many murders is this right worth? And such cases are in fact only a fraction of the damage caused in the exercise of that dubious privilege.

Take the Indiana tragedy, for example. The movie *Helter-Skelter*, which in some way caused the murders, was itself based on the real-life phenomenon of the Manson cult, which in turn was facilitated by the media. (It seems that the Manson group began to initiate acts of violence after Manson heard a Beatles tune called "Helter-Skelter.") By not responding to the ominous warnings of the *Psycho* murders and other episodes, we have created a situation in which art and life are tumbling over each other, with sensationalistic art reflecting the worst qualities of life back onto itself, each making the other worse, until now we have no sense of judgment. We are creating, among other serious and needless problems, people who think killing is fun.

Why do we let this continue? For one thing, the sense of responsibility is not easily aroused in us humans in the best of times; if only a few cases of violence are obviously triggered by the media, who knows what happened in the others? Perhaps the perpetrators just went crazy. But why are the people who are going over the edge, or people close to them, not able to realize themselves what is happening to them? Because it happens slowly. One of the most important studies of the effects of seeing portrayals of violence, television violence in this instance, was carried out by a British psychologist, William Belson. The study took six years to complete and involved him in the lives of 1,565 London teen boys. Belson's graphic term for the way that television produces disinhibition is the "battering-ram effect." With every cowboy or Indian shot down on the screen, an imperceptible but very real degree of inhibition is dissolved in the viewer's mind. If he or she is young, the process happens so much faster (indeed, immediate increases in aggression after each viewing have been measured in other studies). When the battering ram has weakened our sensibilities enough, the violence that we as a human family have labored for evolutionary ages to bring under control breaks out. If by some magic we, or people important to us, could see the transformation, if we could see the persons we are slowly turning into, we would be repelled.

But there is no magic. "Whatever changes are taking place in the boys," says Dr. Belson, "are occurring below the conscious level." And the "horror of television," confirms a prominent EEG specialist, "is that information goes in, but we don't react to it. It goes right into our memory pool and perhaps we react to it later but we don't know what we're reacting to. . . . Later on you're doing things without knowing why you're doing them"—things that range from buying a particular brand of toothpaste to buying a gun. Increases in aggressiveness have been observed up to a decade after the violence was seen.

The real effects of violent entertainment, then, go far beyond giving some tips to those who are already looking for ways to commit a crime or prompting a few people here and there to commit one in direct imitation. Violence in the media gradually makes us more prone to violence in *general*. The effect on Dr. Belson's subjects, as on the boy in my children's high school, was cumulative. What his boys saw on television was reflected outward as a whole range of apparently unrelated acts of aggression, such as "swearing and the use of bad language, aggressiveness in sport or play, threatening to use violence on another boy, writing slogans on walls, breaking windows."

Even this finding does not bring home to us the full human cost of watching violence. It is good to consider how people behave, but the most grievous damage is already taking place inside of them, affecting how they feel. I believe that this was the point of a cartoon that a colleague of mine had for a while on his bulletin board. It showed a line of people queued up for the latest horror movie. The crowd from the previous showing was already pouring out—and quite a crowd it was: reptilian monstrosities of every shape and size, hissing at the astounded customers, "Go back! Go back! We were people, just like you!"

When we lose a measure of feeling for our fellow human beings, we lose part of our humanity. This is alienation. This is "brutalization," as the cartoonist was trying to suggest; and it is emphasized by one of the most important of Belson's findings: that the most harmful *kinds* of violence to see are not those in which physical injury is inflicted but those in which close relationships are violated—hostility among close friends, or between lovers, or between husband and wife. A harsh word, if it attacks such a human bond, can be more destructive than a shootout between cops and robbers that leaves the screen littered with bodies.

To put it in a few words, the effect of violence in the media is precisely to reverse what Einstein called the "task" of every human life: to become progressively more aware of the unity of all life. The presence of violence—that is, in its physical expression—is only one way of measuring the reversal. But violence must result as long as the psychological battering continues. If you recall that the state of mind of people capable of killing causes them to view other human beings as "life-sized dolls," it will shock you to read the description one film critic gave of *Boulevard Nights* and *The Warriors*, the gang warfare films I mentioned at the beginning of this chapter: In these films violence is treated "lyrically," he said; scene after scene consists of actors "like a series of carefully dressed, large-scale dolls mutilating one another." And the results of this misrepresentation of human beings? Here are the exact words of Susan Atkins of the Manson cult: "How could I have felt any emotion without knowing them? They didn't even look like people. . . . I didn't relate to Sharon Tate as being anything but a store mannequin."

WHAT IS TO BE DONE?

If we are tired of making ourselves sick and do not want to feed the hydra-headed monster of violence any longer, only one resource is basic enough and powerful enough to help us: Deep down inside nobody *likes* to be dehumanized. This latent positive capacity within human nature is hinted at, through the veil of humor, in the cartoon I've mentioned, which satirizes the new phenomenon of horror movies. If you think over the implications of films about earthquakes, air crashes, infernos, and things loathsome and disgusting, it is almost as if the producers are telling us, "If you are jaded by anger, fear, and lust, don't despair! Come on in and let us make you sick." And so we do. *Texas Chainsaw Massacre*, for example, was boldly advertised as a film that would nauseate, and it gave eighty people that dubious experience opening night.

Is nausea fun? People can be conditioned to believe so, for given enough time history has shown that people can get used to anything. But at deeper levels, below the conditioning, there remains some recognition that nausea is not fun at all. Neither is "cinematic neurosis," the condition of depressive anxiety induced by this "entertainment," if you ask the San Francisco psychiatrist who has been treating it. We have trained ourselves not to recognize how much alienation hurts. Richard Speck, who "just went crazy" one day in Chicago and killed eight student nurses, is now behind bars, where the authorities let him spend hours in front of a television set watching murder programs—as if the suffering inside him didn't matter. But in fact it matters very much, and we can learn to monitor such suffering long before it forces its way out of us in neurotic symptoms or acts of violence.

I think we all have at some time or another been aware of the unpleasant transformation taking place in us, though there was little support from society to confirm that it was unpleasant and in fact a legitimate danger sign. My wife and I never had a television set. When our children discovered television at our friends' homes they naturally began a regular campaign for us to get them a set "like all the other kids." We got nowhere trying to explain why we did not want to. But one day when we were visiting some close friends, their two children and ours became engrossed in an afternoon program called "Flipper," which is usually suitable for children. On this afternoon, though, when I looked over from our conversation I could see that the children were as if spellbound by fear. On the screen were a boy and a girl adrift off the Florida Keys in a leaky rowboat, while around them circled the telltale dorsal fin of a big shark. The kids on the screen were terrified; and as the shark began to bump against the sinking boat, the children in our warm, dry living room were terrified too. I went over and asked if they wanted to turn the set off. Glassy-eyed, they murmured resistance, and I let them continue.

Some days later—Flipper eventually rescued the Florida children, of course—Jess and Josh came back to their theme: "Why can't we have television like the other kids?"

I simply asked, "Do you remember that program you were watching the other day?"

"Uh-huh."

"Did you like it?"

"No!"

"Could you turn it off when I asked you to?"

"Um, no."

"That's why we're not going to have a television set."

They never raised the question again.

The easy and natural time to stop conditioning is before it starts. Parents are ideally situated to intercept this habituation for their children—the one class for whom such "censorship" is not an obnoxious or undemocratic intrusion. Once the habit has taken root it is of course much more difficult to deal with. "When I watch television I'm bored and yet fixated at the same time," said a man interviewed by television critic Jerry Mander; "I hate what I'm watching. . . but I keep watching anyway."

As adults we may run across expert studies by Alberta Siegel, George Gerbner, Albert Bandura, or others who have demonstrated scientifically that television alienates us from one another, deprives us of freedom of choice, undermines democracy, casts a pall of fear over our lives, and causes us to live with an impoverished, distorted sense of reality. We might read Marie Winn's *The Plug-In Drug*, or see the film

Being There, or, if we're rock fans, hear Frank Zappa sing, "I am the best you can get / Have you guessed me yet? / I am the slime oozin' out / From your TV set"—all of which give television a badly needed drubbing. Or we may hear about the congressional studies of 1954, 1961, 1964, and 1970, and the surgeon general's 1971 report on television and social behavior (all five volumes of it), which came to the same conclusions about television (and other media) violence: "Television enters powerfully into the learning process of children and teaches them a set of moral and social values about violence which are inconsistent with the standards of a civilized society." Should we entertain the thought that viewing violence is some sort of "safety valve" for potentially violent pressures building up within us—the "cathartic" theory—the best evidence in these reports will tell us the much less reassuring truth.

But none of these exposés, not the popular songs or the scientific studies or the government documents or our own common sense, got the government to do anything or—which is more to the point—led ordinary citizens in any appreciable number to reduce the time they spent watching television violence. Why? Because the conditioning is too unconscious, too subliminal, the habit too ingrained to be dislodged simply by knowing the facts. We hate what we're doing, but we do it anyway.

Yet because we are dimly aware that we hate it, we are partly motivated to expel it. All that we need to do is shake ourselves out of our torpor and make an effort to fight back. The next time you have an impulse to turn on the tube, do something else instead, something that is not boring or fixating, something that can give you a "live" connection with real people, such as going for a walk with your family.

It is obvious how much individuals and families could benefit from this simple act of choice. As an experiment, one elementary school in New Jersey told the pupils to do without watching television for a week. In some homes it became clear that the parents, not the children, were the problem. But in others the parents were cooperative, and there, as one eleven-year-old put it simply, "I saw a lot more of my parents, I got to know them a lot more." A mother said, "I don't think any of us will go back to our old habits—either our kids or ourselves." But can such individuals and families, without legal action, change the balance for society as a whole? Can they make a difference to a giant industry that enjoys such hypnotic hold over a nation? Assuredly they can.

The people who profit from violence in the media are not ogres. By and large they are in the business either to make money or to impress us with their creativity. Whatever their motives, they depend on our support.

The head of programming at a major network was asked not long ago to describe the thinking process that led to the network's selection of programs. He fielded the question perfectly: There was no thinking process whatsoever. Television and film producers are notorious for providing whatever fare the ratings and the box offices tell them will generate the most immediate profits. What this produces, of course, is a lowest-common-denominator effect whereby the viewers most susceptible to sensationalism exert a dominant control over the market. Soon they become progressively conditioned to ever cheaper and quicker entertainment "fixes," so that for the studios to maintain profits, their standards must become progressively more vulgar.

The Warriors, one of the "ultraviolent" gang warfare films, resulted almost immediately in six deaths; but it also resulted in a $3½ million gross intake the first *weekend* it was shown. That is why, at this writing, the studio has seven more films of that genre "in the can," most of which may have come your way by the time you read this book.

On the other hand, when the *TV Violence Index* was first published in July, 1976, a number of viewers withdrew their patronage from the ten companies listed as sponsoring the most offensive, violent programs. All ten companies immediately passed the word along to the networks to ease up on the violence.

So it is with all producers: We buy, they produce. We buy differently, they produce differently. Most publishers are the same in this regard. Early in 1977, as if to illustrate this to extremes, a new magazine hit the newsstands: *Assassin, The Secret World of the Killer Elite*. It was a how-to publication, telling how you could build your own atomic bomb or assassinate a head of state. In fact, the cover of the first issue showed President Carter as seen through the crosshairs of a telescopic rifle. The publisher had this to say:

> I realize that the cover is in bad taste, but launching a magazine is a long-term proposition. I'm a real admirer of Carter, but I'm finding in

my travels that there is a real pathological hatred of him among a lot of people. I'm just trying to be realistic. . . . The initial response to *Assassin* is proving that there really is a market for it out there. . . . It's not just the nuts. It's a broad spectrum of Americans, people from all walks of life who want to know about this kind of thing and are curious. . . . It looks like we may make a lot of money off this. It's going to provide us with a very nice living.

What do you do about a man who feels it's just a "living" to exploit people's pathological hatreds or that it's "realistic" to base your life on money? You ignore him. It happens that if *Assassin* fails (and I think it has), the next publishing venture he has in mind is a magazine on early child care. Whether he promotes life or death depends on what we buy.

Actors and writers are no more an obstruction to our intentional changes in the industry than their producers or publishers. Setting aside an occasional John Wayne, no image gives them an inflexible commitment to violence. Some, like Maximilian Schell, just wait for a film with some meaningful purpose to act in. Star of everything from *A Bridge Too Far* to a German version of *Hamlet*, Schell has said somewhere that the only film he feels really good about is one you have probably never heard of, *The Reluctant Saint*, a low-budget drama about Joseph of Cupertino.

This is not the last time in this book we shall conclude that the crucial resource in solving a problem related to violence is released when we arouse the judgment of individuals. I concur with a former editor of the *New England Journal of Medicine* that "only one effective weapon really is available, and that is the boycott." Do not wait for governmental controls to be imposed or for a change of heart in the industry. Withdraw support from what you do not want; give it to what you do want.

One consolation lurks in the fact that government has been unwilling to respond to the dangerous indoctrination of media violence so far. We are still largely free of a most unwanted form of government response—censorship. But no society can tolerate indefinite amounts of violence. No less a libertarian than Walter Lippman has begun to say that the risks to our liberties censorship represents may be soon outweighed by the erosion of those liberties by violent disorder and society's efforts to protect itself by violent forms of order. If we want to *stay* free of censorship, then, we must have self-control. If we do not, our choice will be not freedom or control but control by others or no control at all. Intentional change is the answer compatible with our dignity.

The question that arises, then, is *what* to boycott. Here we have to think both of medium and content. Obviously, violence is the most injurious content; but there may be less obvious content that is just as bad. Remember that we are trying to reverse the process of recent history, returning through today's horror, disaster, and gang warfare movies, through crime, war, and cowboy movies to a state in which human beings were portrayed as treating one another with respect, and with awareness of the dignity and meaning of one another's lives. Not only does this mean the end of violence; it means that pornography has got to go as well. This is not a question of morality. Plenty of recent evidence has shown that pornography, no less than overt violence, can stimulate aggression, because pornography is really a form of violence. Did we not used to call women "dolls" in a sexual context? Anything, including language, that portrays another human being as "other," as an object to be had, mistreated, or enjoyed, can mislead the human mind. If we want to be responsible and effective viewers, what do we do when violence, or sex, or money is being exploited? We walk out.

So much for content. I saw *Psycho* the year it was released in a theater in Bakersfield, California, where it was filmed. I remember how effective it was even there. Today you can see it in your own living room, without having to find a babysitter or park your car, without going anywhere beyond the private world of your own household. The effects of television have been so well written of by Marie Winn, Jerry Mander, Jerzy Kozinski, and others that they need no further elaboration here. Of course television is not the whole problem. You can "just go crazy" from reading magazines if nothing more devastating is available. But for all kinds of reasons—the mesmerization, the passivity, the weird alienation wrought when 40 million people simultaneously watch the same images without talking to one another—I recommend a complete mercy killing for commercial television, at least until such time as we are mature enough to use it wisely. The human race has been around in one shape or other for nearly 5 million years, while television was not even invented until 1923. We can do without it beautifully.

It is not true that violence is mysterious and that nothing can be done about it. We have been overlooking something we can do about it right in our living rooms.

If you are not much of a joiner and do not want to spend your evenings licking stamps for Action for Children's Television or one of the thirty-five other groups that have taken up this problem in an organized fashion, you can still do what many other parents have done for a first step: Stash the tube in the basement until you are ready to get rid of it. You will soon feel free to do the same with other forms of vulgar entertainment and other forms of violence. You will be on your way to expelling the Hydra's poison from your system.

3 | Public Enemy Number One

And it came to pass, when they were in the field, that Cain rose up against Abel, his brother, and slew him.
And the Lord said unto Cain, Where is Abel, thy brother? And he said, I know not: am I my brother's keeper?

Genesis 4:8–9

Every time I see one of those bumper stickers that reads "If It Feels Good, Do It," I imagine I am seeing how we have made our civilization a school for violence. The people who believe in this slogan are free and easy. They are not bad people. They are "anything goes," "laid back," "beautiful" people who can point to the fact that they are only being open about what is secretly everybody's creed. And they honestly believe that if everyone were like them, violence would not be a problem. Yet one of the reasons violence is increasing is precisely that this attitude is becoming more prevalent. "Me-ism" is only separateness in a modern guise, and separateness is alienation by another name.

CIRCLES OF COMPASSION

A human life is played out within various circles—family, community, nation, world. What is our relationship to all these circles, or what should it be? A saying attributed to Confucius runs:

> If there is righteousness in the heart, there will be
>   beauty in the character;
> If there is beauty in the character, there will be
>   harmony in the home;
> If there is harmony in the home, there will be
>   order in the nation;
> If there is order in the nation, there will be
>   peace in the world.

Confucius's model, then, is a kind of centrifugally radiating harmony. All violence ultimately derives from individuals. Likewise, all peace derives from individuals who learn to feel at one with progressively wider circles of humanity around themselves. Just as Einstein said.

Long before Confucius, and before human beings cared much about articulating theories of their own behavior, our prehistoric ancestors may have understood and used this principle. Evidence comes from the way some technologically backward peoples still live today—for example, the Mbuti Pygmies, who still practice a hunter-gatherer economy in the rain forests of central Africa.

The Mbuti raise their children with extreme care and attention to the problem of aggression. At every stage of development, parents see to it that the children do not lose self-control and give way to disruptive, aggressive impulses. A child is nurtured so that the primal security of the mother's womb is carried through all its later growth experiences, expanding with the child to encompass the ever larger and more complex circles of Mbuti culture up to the largest circle a Mbuti will normally encounter, the forest. The primary goal of Mbuti culture, it seems, is to let this circle of security expand without being broken.

Colin Turnbull, the British anthropologist from whom I draw my information, has very sensitively described this process. Long before the child is born, the expectant Mbuti mother picks a spot in the forest and goes there every day to prepare the place for herself, to make it a place where she can feel comfortable and secure. She may lean her back against her favorite tree and rock herself gently while cradling her belly in her hands, singing her baby a lullaby she has composed herself. When she is about to give birth, she goes there either by herself or, if she expects to have problems, with a close friend or two. With rare exceptions she delivers the baby joyfully and easily. She is secure and happy, and she communicates her security to the new arrival.

The umbilical cord is not cut right away, sometimes not for an hour. First the mother places the baby on her abdomen so it can feel the new but familiar-smelling world of her body, until that world seems as safe and close as the womb itself. When it is time to cut the cord, the father and a few other relatives come around. (The father will later be physically experienced in the same way the mother has been when he encourages the infant to nestle on his chest and have its first solid food.)

The Mbuti child spends its first months of life, as it did its first hours, in almost constant reassuring physical contact with the "second womb" of its mother's body. "But then," Turnbull writes, "it is time to be born again, into yet another sphere, that of the *endu*, the dwelling made of forest sticks and leaves." The baby explores this new world as gradually as he has explored his mother's body. When he encounters a sharp thorn or a biting ant, she lets him, but she also lets him come back to comfort in her arms. "Challenge is productive and necessary," Turnbull explains, "but the Mbuti ration it out in doses that never for a moment threaten to destroy the confidence in ultimate success, confidence in the ultimate goodness of the forest/sphere/womb." Thus the security of the womb is neither clung to nor abandoned:

> From the moment of birth onwards everything is done to enable that sense of security to be transferred in steadily widening and inclusive circles from the sphere that is limited to the mother's body to the *endu* (leaf hut), to the *bopi* (playground), to the *apa* (camp) and finally to the most inclusive sphere of all, *ndura* (the forest).

The product of this system is an adult with an "otherwise almost incredible trust and confidence" in his or her human and natural environment. Though the Mbuti have their share of tribal stresses and strains, though they have troubles with agricultural peoples beyond their social sphere, this sense of being at one with the successively surrounding circles in which they live their lives gives them almost complete freedom from human violence.

Different societies, of course, differ in where they draw successive circles of identity. Where the next circle beyond a Mbuti family is the playground, in a Confucian society it might be the extended ancestral family and, beyond that, the patriarchal state. In the industrialized world and particularly North America we have been trying in effect to get by with no circle of identity larger than the family, perhaps none larger than the individual. In our urban culture, the neighborhood (an approximate equivalent of the village) could serve as an important middle ground, a secure place between the now embattled family and the faceless metropolis. But through the last few decades' "unsettling of America," as writer and farmer Wendell Berry calls it, we have broken down traditional circles such as neighborhood, community, and town and created a vast psychological distance between the average individual and the nation state, or some other large, impersonal unit like the corporation. Many individuals cannot cross this gap. All of us suffer to some degree for lack of a mechanism to spread our natural sympathies outward, and of course society suffers too. We are no longer engaged or connected; we feel unwilling to make sacrifices and lack the satisfaction a valid sacrifice can bring. Alienation and, of course, violence result. Interestingly enough, even a little restoration of this sense of community, accomplished by something as simple as a change in traffic patterns, has been found to reduce violence in neighborhoods from California to Connecticut.

Einstein describes our task as "widening our circle of compassion." Albert Schweitzer used virtually the same language: "Until it extends the circle of its compassion to all living things, humanity will not itself find peace." Confucius saw a succession of values—"righteousness," "beauty," "harmony," "order"—as vehicles of this expansion of concern, while for the Mbuti, as Turnbull interprets their experience, what expands is primarily security and a sense of belonging (which ancient philosophers called *oikeōsis*, 'making the world one's home'). Both modern me-ism and all of this collective wisdom begin with the individual, but there the resemblance ends. For me-ism also ends, tragically, with the individual. It goes nowhere, while the horizon Einstein and the others have described goes literally everywhere. Me-ism reverses the direction of human interest; while for the others, whatever differences of language they may employ, the fulfillment of both the individual and society are seen to depend on the individual's ability to *expand* his or her awareness, love, and sense of unity, to embrace more and more of what is "other" as his or her own. But in me-ism all this love and attention shrinks and finally collapses back onto itself. "We are party today," said a pediatrician concerned with the effects of television on the family, "to a widespread cynical retreat into self-centeredness and loss of concern for public needs." That is a formula for violence.

THE FAMILY CIRCLE

The idea of inward and outward direction makes clear at once why the family plays a crucial role in the overcoming of alienation and, hence, of violence. Under normal circumstances the family is—both in time and by psychological geometry—every person's first circle. Will the child learn to think of himself as part of a larger whole, identifying his welfare with that of others by sacrificing the satisfaction of some personal desires in the give-and-take of daily life, or will he remain a separate fragment, locked in a touchy circle of sensitivity that includes only himself? It is in the family that the first steps are taken—steps that determine in large measure how the rest of our life's journey will be walked.

Doctors M. Klaus and J. H. Kennell, pediatricians who have written a well-known manual on infant-parent bonding, describe the relationship between infant and mother as the "wellspring for all the infant's subsequent attachments and the formative relationship in the course of which the child develops a sense of himself." But the quality of this bond, they point out, is itself determined by the quality of the family circle. Even this primal, biological union between mother and child can fail to form as well as it can if both parents do not share a stable love for each other and for the child. Mothers mother their children better if the father is around—and Klaus and Kennell feel that this shows up in the first *hours* after birth.

One would expect disruption in family life to be a strong contributing factor to violence, and this is exactly what social scientists have found. It is important to realize, of course, that for a creature as complex as a human being, biological consanguinity and physical presence are not the whole story. When is a family not a family? For example, when all its members are glued to a television set, not interacting with one another. Young children are particularly affected by such isolation. They have always needed a prolonged period of intimate interaction with caring others to learn how to come out of themselves. Without it, they go into the streets locked into a child's somnambulistic world, unable to play intensely with others, or learn from others, condemned to alienation and all that follows. In families where the electronic invader has been pushed out, people notice immediately how much more *sociable* they become: "The biggest difference was that we began to do a lot of talking together. It was like old-fashioned living, somehow. The four of us sat around and just talked about everything. We talked and talked."

Scientists have long known that newborn monkeys often die if separated from their mothers, no matter how well their physical needs are provided for. On the other hand, even a stuffed doll if made of soft material can be enough of a substitute "mother" to pull a neglected baby monkey through. Human beings, however, need better nurturing. In a statistical study of newborn infants left in foundling homes it was found that many of them "failed to thrive." Infants deprived of physical contact and mothering were damaged irreparably. (Indeed, in one home thirty-four out of ninety-one infants actually died.) In those instances where substitute mothers provided close attention, infants did thrive, on the whole. For humans, then, "family" is any setting of close, personal relationships in which bonds of deep trust and mutual responsibility are formed. And family is what gives us the security we must have to expand the circle of our compassion.

We can watch this expansion working in a rather atypical example, the famous case of Roseto, Pennsylvania. Roseto was selected as a data base for medical and insurance statistics, because it had the appealing look of a typical American town. It took the insurance companies months to figure out what was going wrong with their calculations: Roseto, population 3,500, was not at all typical. The inhabitants of Roseto, though they had the same bad diet most Americans have and much the same lack of exercise, did not at all have the same rate of heart disease. Other diseases also turned out to be less frequent and less fatal. Not only that, when sociologists started checking further they discovered less crime and virtually no poverty in Roseto. The reason? Roseto was largely settled by Italians, and Italians have traditionally structured their social life in terms of large, extended families. All the inhabitants had a neighborly concern for one another, primarily because the "family," as psychologist James Lynch put it, was "the focus of life there." This did not mean that if you were not a member of a family (or an Italian) you were ostracized in Roseto. But family *values* radiated outward from the family centers of Roseto into the larger circles of the neighborhood and the whole "body politic" of the town, the way life-nourishing order spreads mysteriously from genes to cells, to organs, to the whole organism. "Nature has many ways to shorten the lives of lonely people," says Lynch, commenting on the higher morbidity of the same diseases among people who have no close friends or kin. In Roseto nobody was lonely.

The Mbuti have a myth about a girl who was abandoned by the tribe and left to grow up alone in the forest. She survives, their story goes, but she turns into a demon who kills people that stray across her path. This parable has meaning for us now. Someone who knew Dan White, the assassinator of Mayor Moscone of San Francisco, commented after the crime, "Dan was basically a loner." Loneliness, a scourge of our times, does a lot of damage to the human being before it shows up as physical symptoms. When it gets too severe, loneliness can breed violence, perhaps as a desperate attempt to create human contact. But who is totally free of loneliness? The only thing that prevents chaos is that, as Professor Boulding says, in *most* people it rarely rises to such violent, desperate levels.

LIFE ON THE BELL CURVE

Psychologists can identify certain types of people who are more likely than others to get provoked into committing a murder or some other violent crime–lacking in impulse control, "hyperthymic" (prone to emotional outbursts), insecure–but they can seldom predict which individuals will actually commit a murder. Murderers have no absolute distinguishing characteristics. What goes out of control in them is lurking in us; what is vestigial in them–self-control, a sense of respect– is not always highly developed in "normal" people either.

Imagine that we could plot on a graph the number of people in a given population who would commit murder (or other violent acts) with progressively increasing provocation. The line on our graph would probably describe a bell curve such as we are familiar with in statistical studies (see Fig. 1). On the far left, where the line slopes off gracefully almost to zero, would be those pathological few whose threshold is by now so low that they are ready to commit murder for practically no reason (say, because you cut in front of them on a freeway); on the far right, where the line similarly drops off, are those happy few like Mahatma Gandhi, who would not commit murder for virtually any reason whatsoever. And mounded up in the center would be the rest of us.

Now let's imagine a vertical line indicating a cutoff point on the curve: Everyone falling to the left of the line *would* commit murder this year given the currently "normal" amount of provocation you can expect in our society. This line would shift to the right or to the left as

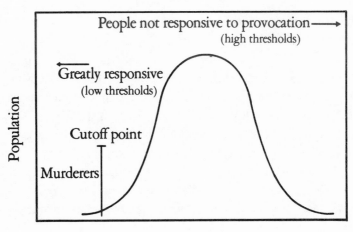

Increasing provocation

FIGURE 1

the various factors that produce fluctuations in the homicide rate rise and fall. At present the line for our population would of course fall well to the left of the crown of the curve (far less than half of us are murderers). Probably it would be somewhere in the area where the curve has begun to rise up sharply to the right, though, so that a small shift of the line to the right or left would mean a large increase or decrease in the number of people included—in other words, a large increase or a dramatic decrease in the homicide rate. And now imagine that from year to year something is pushing that line slowly but surely to the *right*. What we would see is exactly what the accompanying graph (Fig. 2) from the National Center for Health Statistics reveals: There has been, starting in the 1960s, a drastically rapid increase in the national homicide rate.

What is eating away at our ability to tolerate frustration, making ever greater numbers of ordinary people into killers? In the simplest terms it is a gradual erosion of respect for life. As our collective capacity to respect the lives of others rises or falls, we can expect a corresponding fall or rise in the physical expressions of indifference—not only in matters such as assault or murder but also in the routine events of everyday life.

Seldom in the history of this country has respect for life been so

FIGURE 2

depleted. If Rip Van Winkle had been asleep for the last twenty years, he would be shocked to hear the cynicism we take for granted from radio announcers, or shopkeepers, the sarcastic disregard in what pass for friendly conversations. The unwritten headline that would convey the message of virtually everything the papers choose to tell us (and we choose to read) is, "Life Is Cheap."

This is not a question of taste, but a failure of culture and of society, fraught with consequences for the quality, not to mention the continuance, of life. Albert Schweitzer said this very well: "Reverence for life is where religion and philosophy can meet and where society must try to go."

In trying not to go that way, seduced perhaps by the glitter of personal freedom that carelessness for values and responsibility may seem to offer, we go right into violence. A Brooklyn psychiatrist, Dr. Denise Shine, cited three elements in the personality of remorseless teenage violent offenders. Lack of respect was first; next came inability to sense the subjective nature of another person's experience; then impatience. In Shine's words, they evidence a "total lack of guilt and respect for life. To them another person is a thing. They are wild organisms who cannot allow anything to stand in their way."

It is no mystery how this "new breed" of remorseless youth has sprung up in our midst; as James Baldwin says, they are simply "imitating our disrespect" for the feelings of other people. You could say that a particular murder is caused on one level by a tendency toward aggression that all human beings inherit. On other levels it is caused by the artificial arousal of that tendency, for example, through violent entertainment; by the inability to relate to others as fellow human beings; by the availability of a "Saturday night special"; by someone who annoys a potential murderer once too often. But it is useful to remember that all these factors have to do with our respect for life. Turn down the dial controlling that crucial value, and the vertical line we were imagining on our bell curve *must* shift to the right. Episodes of violence must become more easily precipitated and more frequent. For statistical reasons, as our curve shows, if this process goes on too long there will be times—and ours is one of them—when the rise in murders will be exponential.

Why is respect for life of such direct importance in violence? Because, as Dr. Shine implies, to respect life is to draw closer to life in general and thus become more sympathetic toward all living creatures. J. B. S. Haldane, one of the greatest natural scientists of our time, once said that "anyone who has the concrete and detailed notion of the unity of life, at which I have arrived after studying biology for sixty years, will at least have some respect for all life." The converse is also true.

It was with sure insight that the Nobel committee gave the prize for peace to Mother Teresa of Calcutta, who had never negotiated a treaty, never, like Betty Williams and Mairead Corrigan the following year, started a movement labeled anything like "peace," but who, in the words of the committee chairman, "promotes peace in the most fundamental manner—by her confirmation of human dignity." The question for us all is whether this insight will remain a matter for lip service and occasional prizes or, as Schweitzer said it must, light up the path for all society to follow. As she stood in Oslo and accepted the prize "in the name of the poor," an ecstatic Bengali said, "Now the Mother of Bengal is the Mother of the world!" But the world has got to make that literally true if it wants to make a break with violence.

Compassion and a sense of our responsibility for others are similar bridges we can use to bring about a desirable expansion of our life into theirs. "Com-passion" literally means feeling with. When psychologist D. W. Johnson investigated some unusually cooperative children, he found that they were "better able to identify how others were feeling and to explain why they were feeling that way." These capacities heal alienation. They are all intimately related and of necessity ebb and flow together in social changes. We hear many cries today for greater "accountability," but this cannot solve the problems caused by the ebb of responsibility and other uniting values: Where responsibility, like compassion and respect, unites people, imposing accountability from without tends to divide them.

And now we can return to the question with which we began this chapter. Why are all these unifying values receding? Obviously, because they have to make room for number one. Though vigorously seeking our own self-interest may seem to be an enlightened way of enhancing our own dignity and through it the dignity of others (a kind of personal "What's good for GM is good for the nation"), it actually does neither. Having fun and feeling good—number one's main ways of knowing he or she is making it—are not the stuff of human dignity. Likewise to "seek your own space" is merely a euphemism for bulldozing others out of your circle of concern. These are not values that make life worth preserving.

Though we think of murder as an act of aggression against others, it is an interesting fact that the suicide rate normally rises or falls in concert with the rate of homicide. Psychologists have discovered in many ways that people who can do violence to others are doing violence to themselves. "It is a terrible, an inexorable law," declared James Baldwin, "that one cannot deny the humanity of another without diminishing one's own."

Ultimately there is no such thing in life as separate advantage. It is an illusion. It is a great irony that almost all the advantages sought by number one are sought in the name of freedom—the freedom to do as one likes. But how can isolation ever bring us freedom? There is no such thing as freedom *from* responsibility. Flight from responsibility takes us not toward freedom but toward a crabbed existence, self-exiled at the margins of reality. Responsibility, far from an encumbrance, is a way of getting into relatedness with our fellow beings, hence a path into the order of being, in which alone our freedom can be realized. Architects designing a housing project in Nuremberg gave the children vast outdoor areas to run around in, to give them freedom. Psychologists discovered later that the children grew up feeling *cramped*. Apart from their parents for long hours, able to separate from one another whenever they had quarrels instead of having to work out the inevitable problems of childhood relationships, they became not free but psychologically constricted. Iron bars do not a prison make, we might say. But alienation does.

The "space" that children—and adults—need to grow up in is provided by relationships. It is not physical territory, not the "space" we glibly refer to in psychobabble, a space that is evacuated of concern for others so that we can do whatever we want; it is the exact opposite: involvement. People need people.

In adult life the responsibility we voluntarily assume for others is a way to gain this vital space. Nothing else explains as well the fulfillment found by such people as Pastor André Trocmé and the members of his parish of Le Chambon sur Ligny, who during the entire occupation of France continued rescuing refugees under the noses of the Gestapo, seeking no reward either then or later but the reward of being, as they called themselves, *les responsables*, "the responsible ones"; and Raoul Wallenberg, who similarly rescued vast numbers of Hungarian Jews with whom he had no particular affiliation.

Responsibility for one another is a need of our species, to be ranked with our need for food and air. Psychoanalyst Viktor Frankl proposed that in addition to the Statue of Liberty on the East Coast, to which he has no objection, this country should erect a Statue of Responsibility on the West Coast. Without responsibility, no liberties can have much meaning. Indeed the "liberty" to isolate ourselves from one another is disguised tyranny. It is not a coincidence that in the Hebraic vision that has given so much light to Western civilization, the first murder, the archetype for all acts of human violence, is simultaneously a profound rejection of kinship and of responsibility: "Am I my brother's keeper?"

Traditional wisdom is important for a very simple reason: Without it we have only our own sense of things to fall back on, and the individual's own light has never been that reliable. If people had nothing but their private feelings to go on, how many of us would take responsibility for the 1½ billion hungry people on this planet, or for those whom our covert exploitation has delivered up to the "strong men" of Latin America, or for those in our own society, the so-called criminal element, who have ended up on the wrong side of the cutoff line on the bell curve?

As for the individual, doing what feels good can result at the most physical level in self-destructive addictions. Death is a hard teacher. Adin Ballou, a nineteenth-century apostle of nonviolence, put it this way: "It is not man's imaginations, thoughts and feelings that determine what is injurious to him" but nature—physical and other laws.

Moods, conditioning, personal urges, and selfish fears, the stimuli of the advertiser—none of these can be a reliable guide for any action. And the prevailing myth of individual fulfillment condemns us to follow just these shaky guides. Where we need to learn from one another, we are told, "Shrink into yourself; number one knows all." Where we need disciplined reflection to piece together the meaning of our experiences or predict the long-range consequences of our actions, the prevailing myth counters, "Just do what feels good *now*." Where we need sensitivity to others, we are advised, "Forget it; number one is the measure of all things."

Poor number one! Shrinking into the smallest circle of awareness, shut up in a narrow private world of his own making, he has nothing to go on but what feels good to him, from moment to moment. How can he know any better? He is promised every satisfaction; indeed, he is urged to claim it as his right—"I want it all, and I want it now!" When life does not deliver—How could it?—is it any wonder that he becomes ever more frustrated, angry, and insecure?

In the last pages of his classic *Mutual Aid: A Factor in Evolution*, Kropotkin reminisces about his visit to a fishing village on the west coast of England at the end of the last century. The villagers had a tradition of trying to rescue whatever survivors they could from the terrible storms that drove ships against the rocks that lay just off their coast. After one occasion Kropotkin asked one of the men why they had attempted something so dangerous when no law or possible gain compelled them to. The villager said that they had hesitated for a long time by the gunwales of their small boats. "Then," he said, "all of a sudden, through the storm, it seemed to us as if we heard their cries—they had a boy with them. We could not stand that any longer. All at once we said, 'We must go!'"

This is a human feeling. In a modern city, in contrast, we have all heard of instances when crowds have stood around and ogled when someone was suffering, or being attacked, or threatening to jump off a building.

For the one question that, if any, matters the most in life—whether the circle of our compassion will expand or contract, whether we save people, abandon them, or become a menace to them—raw feelings are wildly erratic guidelines for behavior. We need something more reliable, something to test our feelings and attitudes against, something that we can use joyfully when we find our feelings wanting. That thing can only be the great model of the unity of life; and we are close now to understanding how we can turn that model into a practical strategy.

When you think about the bell-curve effect, by which any erosion of human dignity must result in violence, no matter how apparently unrelated, an embarrassing question emerges: How much violence do we want? How many murders are we willing to endure so that some people can watch all the violent entertainment they want? Obviously, when the question is posed that way, we want no violence at all. Any attempt to weigh the value of human lives against a privilege so dubious is bound to strike us as grotesque.

And remember that violence is a Hydra-headed monster, so that the question repeats itself in many other aspects of public and private policy. But uncomfortable as it may make us, it is only by facing the question *wherever it appears* that we begin to discern a guideline and a strategy for winning the battle against violence.

For example, in the United States we put up with a "certain number" of traffic fatalities every year (in 1979 the toll was 51,083). In other words, we pay a price for our way of life, which is more deaths every year than the entire toll of combat fatalities in the Vietnam war. *Is it worth it?* It is a question we have never debated, but the question is still there.

And because it is there, Herman Kahn, then head of Rand Corporation, was able to justify the approach of his institute when it calculated the number of "megadeaths" we would suffer in various kinds of nuclear attack and how many years it would take the economy to recover. Many people found this approach revolting, but he had a point. If we set a price on the value of life, why can't he do some quantitative juggling with that price?

Another example of this inconsistency on our part can be seen in the case of Dan White, who murdered Mayor George Moscone and Supervisor Harvey Milk of San Francisco over a personal grievance. The shocked reaction of the press was, Why? Why had this "all-American boy" suddenly turned to violence and caused his city such grief? The answer lay in the very things that we Americans consider today to be all-American, the things that made Dan White seem to us so normal and reliable. He had been a paratrooper, had fought for his country in Vietnam, had been a policeman and a boxer. He voted for the death penalty. Did Dan White really "turn to violence"? Or did he just turn to a kind of violence we don't like? We approved of violence as a means of controlling the "criminal element"; we found a place for it in sports and entertainment. We regarded violence against the Vietnamese (the North Vietnamese, when you could tell the difference) as permissible. In a word, we accepted violence, and we got violence. This is why my graduate student who believed in "controlled violence" was so tragically wrong. Once the beast is let in, no one can control its biting.

The answer to our awkward question is unavoidable. The value of human life is not negotiable. If a television program under consideration may prompt a few unstable individuals out of 200 million to commit murder, that price is too high to pay. Any loophole, any hairline stress can become a crack in the dike through which violence will begin to seep into all levels of society. We will not start to reverse the present trend toward violence until we decide that we want violence not contained, not reduced, not controlled, but *eliminated*.

The strategy we are looking for, then, takes the form of an act of will and a decision: There must be no more violence. We will renounce all violent entertainment even if what we are left with is parlor games. We will accept no traffic deaths but if need be will set to work figuring out how to run our lives without highways. We will not rest with a social system that requires a "little," controlled, violent retribution but will build toward a society in which no one becomes criminal in the first place. We will use no violence to exert our national will on other countries but if necessary will work out an entirely different way to get along with them. That is the challenge.

At the root of all these great changes is the greatest and most difficult of all: serving notice on number one. As long as number one is sovereign, what is the difference between the (North) Vietnamese enemy and the mayor enemy? The urge to be always "feelin' good" must be absorbed by the drive to work on the task that Einstein identifies, that of constantly expanding our circle of sensitivity to include the needs of others. All personal feelings may have to be subordinated to, if not replaced by, the deeper currents of compassion, respect, and responsibility that bind our lives to those of others. In the end, me-first has got to become me-last.

To eliminate all violence, even down to its secret nesting places in ourselves, is of course a high ideal. But as we have seen, a high ideal is precisely what we need to escape the tyranny of our lower feelings. Such an ideal does not imply a timetable, and it is not a prediction. I, for one, have no idea when or even whether domestic violence or war or ecological degradation or all of these will destroy us before we destroy the hydra that spawns them. But the ideal of no violence, zero violence, is one we can hold before us the way God, according to Plato, slapped up a blueprint of the universe, which he keeps glancing up at during his ongoing work of dissolution and creation.

If you remember the enormity of the outrage that is being perpetrated against life, it will not seem strange that a major overhaul of our modern outlook may be necessary to counter it. So far, in this twentieth century, nearly 1 million American civilians have been shot to death by their fellow Americans, more than all the military personnel killed in action in all the foreign wars this country has ever engaged in. If me-firstism has been implicated in this tragedy, then that value system is ready for the oblivion of the dinosaurs. And to convince you that it *is* implicated, let me conclude this chapter with the following observations.

One winter evening in 1972, two men came into the Weinsteins' neighborhood bakery in Brooklyn and asked for apple pie.

"Sorry," Mr. Weinstein said, "we're out of apple pie just now." At that, one man pulled out a gun and shot Mr. Weinstein dead.

This case is of course extreme. Such people are lunatics, out of their minds, nothing like the majority of us easy-going people, who would never kill anyone over a piece of pie. Besides, look at the other factors: cheap, readily available handguns, racial tension (the customers were black and the Weinsteins, Jewish), a rumor that the Weinsteins had had dealings with racketeers. Agreed. Yet do not all of these contributing factors have a common element: separate individuals or separate groups taking their own interests as supreme and the interests of others as inconsequential?

Even if this is an extreme case, there is still something typical about it. Think of the rash of violent outbursts all around the country four years later, during the first gas shortage. In one case, a man in Alameda, California, got so angry at an attendant who refused to sell him more than his share that he came back with his shotgun and killed the man. Another lunatic? All right, but not at all the only one. A decade beyond 1972, and we read about incidents like this almost every day. And it's hard to ignore the similarity between this way of dealing with frustration and the State Department's dark hints to certain Middle Eastern nations that military force "could not be ruled out" if they tried to withhold our oil. ("Our" oil, indeed.)

Unless it is checked or mitigated, the creed of "me" cannot but lead to violence, for whether the me in question is a person or a nation-state, me-firstism is separateness, and separateness is the root condition of violence.

"I knew it was right, because it felt good when I was doing it." Those dreadfully familiar words are once again from Susan Atkins, member of the Manson cult, telling how she murdered Sharon Tate when the latter was eight months pregnant.

Part Two

IS ZERO VIOLENCE POSSIBLE?

4 | The Answer of Evolution

Life is an aspiration; man is not man as yet.

Robert Browning

Man is not complete; he is yet to be.

Rabindranath Tagore

Over the past twenty years or more I have found myself discussing nonviolence with every imaginable sort of person—fellow academics, students, career State Department officials, friends, children, former political cronies, an uncle, draft board officials, to name a few. It has always amazed me that no matter who they are, the people who resist the idea of nonviolence eventually come up with the same objection: "You can't change human nature."

That objection has never seemed less valid to me. Think of how much we have changed that most fundamental of human relationships, the relationship between man and woman. Today a woman can be a bank president or a garage mechanic or join the army; a man who wouldn't have been caught dead doing it ten years ago can take up knitting or stay home with the baby. Did these changes in behavior require a change of human nature? If so, then human nature can be changed. If not, then it's not necessary to change human nature to change the behavior and thought patterns that lead to violence, either.

THE EYE OF THE ELEPHANT

Gandhi said, "Let no man dogmatise about the capacity of human nature for degradation or for exaltation." What is human nature? How do we know what human beings are endowed with?

There was a time, according to Plato, before any mortal creatures had come into existence. At the appointed hour for their creation, the gods made up their basic forms out of earth and fire and "whatever [was] soluble in these two ingredients" and appointed the brothers Prometheus and Epimetheus to equip the new creations for survival. Epimetheus got his brother's permission to try his hand at the job himself, and in most respects he did very well. To some creatures he allotted weapons such as teeth and claws; to others he gave the ability to run fast or fly or burrow in the ground. He made sure the carnivores would not be too prolific, but he allowed their prey to have many offspring so that one way or another every species could survive.

Then came the hitch. Planning ahead had never been Epimetheus's strong point (his name, in fact, means "afterthought"). He distributed all the evolutionary advantages he had to the nonrational animals, and when it came time to consider human beings there was no capacity for survival left to give them. When Prometheus arrived to look the job over, he found a hairless, unshod animal with blunt teeth and no claws—in short, with no way to defend itself and get on in the world on which the gods were about to raise the curtain of creation. Prometheus, always the resourceful one (his name means "forethought"), had to slip into the workshop of the gods and steal two powers from Hephaestus and Athena: technology and "fire" (what we call energy).

With these two divine advantages, human creatures did fairly well for some time in their competition with the other animals. But they could not get along with one another, and their disorganization left them defenseless. Every time some of them tried to band together and build cities to protect themselves and their works from predatory animals, they fell to fighting and killing one another instead. Prometheus had not been clever enough. The human species was its own worst enemy.

Zeus was annoyed. He saw that this species, unlike all the others, was headed for extinction. So he had to send Hermes with instructions to give them two more precious skills: respect and justice.

"Do I give it to all of them," asked Hermes, "or only a few professionals?"

"To all of them," Zeus said, "and make a law that those who do not take their share of respect and justice should be done away with as a plague to civilization." And so it was. Armed with respect for one another and the capacity to discriminate right from wrong, human beings were able to build civilized communities and not only survive but rise to the lofty heights of Plato's time.

Despite its simple exterior, this sophisticated little story says a great deal about the nature of *Homo sapiens*. While by no means belittling technology and energy, which it acknowledges to be gifts (however unwilling) of the gods, it shows the uselessness of these gifts without the precious ability to cooperate. And the skills that allow us to cooperate, the story says—here anticipating an insight that was formulated only after many decades of Darwinism—are the specific, definitive characteristics of human nature. Without them, we would not be human.

Natural history bears out these insights. We have come to recognize that sociability—the ability of members of a species to cooperate—is perhaps the greatest of all evolutionary advantages. Rudimentary forms of it, we now know, informed evolutionary progress long before the emergence of the specifically human sensitivities to respect and justice. A research team of California zoologists and biochemists has calculated that mammals evolved ten times faster as a result of their ability to form "extended families" of herds and packs. Without that ability we would still be at the level of the opossum. On the other hand, we all know to our cost that technology can be a dubious blessing if we rely on it instead of on our capacity for cooperation for solving social problems. An early naturalist, by way of example, pointed out somewhere that sociable animals like the ants he was observing in Brazil were providing themselves with better housing, all things considered, than the hovels thrown together by *Homo sapiens* in the nearby slums.

Since World War II, people at peace marches the world over have been holding up placards with a big picture of a dinosaur and the motto, "Extinct—Too Much Armor, Too Little Brain." Indeed, the arms race, when you stop to think about it, is our most flagrant attempt to solve a problem of relationships not with the forces that improve relationships, like respect and justice, but with technology. It is an evolutionary throwback.

No one has a complete answer to the question, What is human nature? but two things are clear: Man's practice of cooperation, that potent evolutionary force, leaves considerable room for improvement; his potential for cooperation is in a league entirely by itself. Who else, through shared culture and an appropriate use of technology, can think in terms of global communication? Who else can think in terms of global law and a global order of governance? This is the direction in which the evolution of human nature has come, and the direction in which it still has far to go. We know that a man or woman can be physically mature but not emotionally mature. Similarly, even the most "developed" nations can behave like children. As Norman Cousins once observed:

> The fact that a combination of adolescent taunting and dangerous irrationality should figure in the behavior of nations may seem ludicrous, but nations involved in confrontation situations exhibit all the petulance, arbitrariness, irrationality and false pride associated with the immature mind. . . . No ego is more powerful than group ego.

Is it implausible, then, that the human race as a whole should still have some growing up to do?

In the early years of this century in a landmark decision on the Eighth Amendment, Supreme Court Justice McKenna referred to the "evolving standards of decency that mark the progress of a maturing society." Neither further physical development of the human body nor new technologies have much to do with this maturation. We have made good use of our opposable thumbs and "fire"; we have not begun to touch our legacy of "respect and justice." There's an old saying in India that the elephant, huge creature that it is, has no idea of its great size because its eyes are so disproportionately small. We too see ourselves as ridiculously small when we think we are physical creatures, dependent on brute strength or machinery. Let us not allow modern conditioning to reduce, instead of liberate, our vision of the possible.

ARE WE VIOLENT BY NATURE?

The debate over whether people are basically good or evil has been going on since the beginning of recorded history. In the first 300 or 400 years A.D. it was waged between the Manicheans and the Pelagians; in the eighteenth century it was renewed in different terms by thinkers like Hobbes and Rousseau. In our age, the frame of reference is no longer religious or philosophical, but scientific. The general public has been unduly influenced by one side of this argument, the side that is not only less scientific and less true, but also (like all things that are less true) more dangerous. The dangerous side of the argument runs more or less like this: "Nature is red in tooth and claw. Man is a product of nature. Therefore..." To quote the exact words of the most influential popular exponent of this argument: "The human being, in the most fundamental aspects of his soul and body, is nature's last, if temporary word on the subject of the armed predator. And human history has to be read in those terms.... Man has emerged from the anthropoid background for one reason only: because he was a killer."

Much conditioning has gone into our passive acceptance of this view of human nature. My generation, for example, was brought up on Superman and Tarzan. We read over and over in the thrilling books of Edgar Rice Burroughs how the great hero of the jungles would "leap to his feet beside the corpse of his foe, and placing one foot upon the broken neck, lift his voice in the hideous challenge of the victorious bull-ape." Now the number of people who have heard this blood-curdling cry in the real jungle, as opposed to the jungles of the untamed imagination, is small. Fighting between real apes, whether you call them bull-apes or not, is rare, and more than 90 percent of the fights observed are settled—as they are among virtually all animals—by display, threat, gesture, and noises, without ever coming to open conflict, much less to fatality. It always amazed Jane Goodall how minutes after a flurry of "war" between chimpanzees and baboons in the Gombe forest, both would be calmly munching bananas side by side with their hair back in place and nobody the worse for wear. By such accounts, Eskimos who settle arguments by song contests are in harmony with nature, while the street fighters of the asphalt jungles—or the Joint Chiefs of Staff at a war meeting—are not.

There *is* violence in nature, but it has been exaggerated. There is also cooperation and a rudimentary kind of nonviolence in nature, which has been overlooked. I once saw a documentary on baboons filmed and narrated by a prominent primatologist. (Studying baboons can help us reconstruct human evolution because their behavior is thought to resemble that of our hominid ancestors. They are highly social animals who come down from the trees by day to forage in the open savannas.) As the camera followed the troop on its daily round, the baboons did at times behave for all the world like a band of people. At one point something sent a wave of agitation through the group; the males bared their teeth, jumped up and down, and made threatening noises at one another, with their hair standing on end to make them look bigger than they were. The narrator said, "Something has made the males angry." Soon afterward they were shown in more peaceful occupations, playing and grooming one another; there was even what looked like kissing and hugging. Here the narrator's comment was, "Now the baboons are exhibiting signs of affectionate behavior."

It may strike you, as it eventually did me, that there's a subtle but important difference between *being* angry and only *exhibiting signs* of affectionate behavior, a difference that came entirely from the mind of the observer. Before he ever saw a baboon, he must have felt that an animal feels anger but is not capable of affection, even though it goes through the motions of affectionate behavior as a signal to its cospecifics. Yet the evidence for both emotions was the same. The scientist's differential valuing of that evidence came from a bias no more scientific than our own: We all know the usefulness to the individual of anger and aggression, but we have hardly given any thought to the usefulness of affection and cooperation. So, without much reflection, we all tend to think that affection has no evolutionary significance. Nothing could be further from the truth; but nothing could be closer to the biases toward aggression we all share, scientist and layperson alike. So we all continue to see life as more ruthless than it really is, even if we get advanced degrees in history or watch baboons for 100 years.

The concept of nature's way as a ruthless survival of the fittest is a crassly oversimplified form of Darwinism (never intended by the great man himself) that has been used to justify everything from the excesses of robber barons to fascism. It is still being used to justify doing nothing about violence. When you stop to think about it, the advantages to nature of even a rudimentary peaceableness are obvious. A species that has no way to check its aggression, as Konrad Lorenz has shown and *Homo sapiens* may be on the verge of demonstrating, will soon destroy itself. A wolverine can kill a rabbit in a trice; but is the ecosystem filled with vicious loners like the wolverine or by millions of "helpless" rabbits? Yet it was the "gladiatorial view" of Darwin's theory that gained the imaginations of illustrious figures such as T. H. Huxley and most of the naturalists and philosophers of the day.

Most—but not quite all. Some naturalists at the end of the last century did not find that an unrelieved competitive struggle was nature's only selection process for the development of species. Instead, they came to the conclusion that cooperation was if anything the stronger operative factor in the process of evolution among animals.

Peter Kropotkin was the most influential of this group. In *Mutual Aid* (1902), he argued on the basis of extensive firsthand observations and prodigious reading that the "mutual aid factor" has been and remains stronger than the "struggle of each against all" in evolution:

> Sociability is as much a law of nature as mutual struggle.... Those animals which acquire habits of mutual aid are undoubtedly the fittest. They have more chances to survive, and they attain, in their respective classes, the highest development of intelligence and bodily organiza-tion.... We may safely say that mutual aid is as much a law of animal life as mutual struggle, but that, as a factor of evolution, it most probably has a far greater importance, inasmuch as it favors the development of such habits and characters as insure the maintenance and further development of the species, together with the greatest amount of welfare and enjoy-ment of life for the individual, with the least waste of energy.

But Kropotkin, whose holistic style of thought is coming into its own today, was much more than a naturalist. The philosopher in this former aristocrat and military officer saw, as Plato had seen, that the forces which brought us up from the animal condition are still in play, checking the counterforces which threaten to reverse that progress:

> In our mutual relations every one of us has his moments of revolt against the fashionable individualistic creed of the day, and actions in which men are guided by their mutual aid inclinations constitute so great a part of our daily intercourse that if a stop to such actions could be put all further ethical progress would be stopped at once. Human society itself could not be maintained for even one single generation.

To repeat, there *is* violence in nature. Predators do kill their prey; males of the same species occasionally kill one another in the course of establishing territory, sexual primacy, or some other form of domi-nance. But what is much more noteworthy than the violence in nature is the extent to which it is held in check, the extent to which such impulses as aid and cooperation have been essential for the survival of individuals, species, and life itself. "The central problem to be solved," says the dean of the new discipline of sociobiology, Edward O. Wilson, "before the behavior of any social species—including human society, most of all human society—can be comprehended, turns out to be *altruism*." It is surprising to find an "ethical" word like "altruism" in the working jargon of contemporary biology, but it has in fact become indispensable, since it describes a behavior that is as near to being universal as anything else in nature. Why do antelope sacrifice themselves for their cospecifics? No, nature is not simply "red in tooth and claw." And that brings us to the second limb of the syllogism: Is man simply a product of nature?

Those who believe that *Homo sapiens* is a hereditary killer argue that nature transmitted her nasty habits to us through what are usually called instincts. It used to be argued that this transmission was part of our genetic make-up, but the connection between the genome (an individual's genetic complement) and behavior seems so tenuous at this time that nothing can be gained by trying to discuss it. "We have very little direct evidence about the genetics of behavior in humans," writes Harvard geologist Stephen Gould, "and we know no way to obtain it." What is more, the whole idea that there are inherited instincts that an animal—leave aside a man or a woman—must blindly follow has proved unsupportable. "The idea that there is anything in any organism, especially in humans, whether in the genes or in anything else, that determines fixed action patterns is rejected by most students of behavior," who stopped using the word "instinct" years ago because it can be so misleading.

It is generally agreed that human babies arrive in the world virtually devoid of functioning instincts, apart from the rooting reflex and the sucking response. Richard Leakey points out that even the sucking response can be affected by experiences, including what the baby has experienced in the womb. Within a day or two after birth the baby can recognize the smell of its mother's milk; within a week or two it knows the sound of her voice and the look of her face. Even for such rudimentary behavior as nursing, then, instincts are joined almost immediately by far more complex and conscious mechanisms—eighteen years before most humans will be called upon to vote, or to join the army, or start a family.

It is therefore a great oversimplification to ask, as a scientist did recently, "Are we to believe that such an immense biological gap exists between us and the other species that nothing at all has been left of our biological heritage?" Of course something has been left; but hasn't something also been added? Doesn't our legacy of capacities for reason, respect, and justice mean that we get to decide how that earlier legacy should express itself in us?

The question is important enough to merit a further look at the scientific evidence. The muscles that control the facial expressions of a monkey, for example, are ennervated almost entirely from a region low down on the brain stem, a region that developed very early in evolution; that is to say, most of the facial expressions of a monkey are autonomic in their neural origin, like the "smile" of an infant having gas pains. In a human being, the same muscles receive 90 percent of their nerve supply from centers much higher, in the cerebral cortex. On one level the grimace of a monkey and of a person may both translate into a roughly similar signal, such as "I threaten you." But the meaning of the human expression can be infinitely more complex—one reason why Leonardo did not choose a monkey to sit for the Mona Lisa.

A further comparison brings out the evolutionary rise of freedom from simple physical determinism more clearly. At the base of the mammalian brain are subcortical centers that are sometimes carelessly said to "control" responses such as aggression. But whether they produce aggression or not depends very much on what species of mammal you are. If one stimulates the amygdala of a cat, it will attack anything in sight. The same nucleus stimulated in a rhesus monkey will cause it to attack only another monkey that it has learned through experience it can dominate (if there are only more dominant monkeys around, it may end up cowering under a table or show other, nonaggressive reactions). In human beings, stimulating any brain center produces reactions even more complex and unpredictable. One woman subject reported that she had felt like slapping the investigator; yet she did not. The human being has a choice.

Proponents of the man-the-killer school have made the mistake of looking exclusively at the *vestigial* human being. Naturally they think that a man or woman must obey this vestige of biological aggression, because that is all they see. They never think of the resources we may have acquired to redirect or counteract our aggressive impulses. Of course, to think of them does raise a difficult question.

In Chapter 1 I mentioned the title of a book, *Living with Terrorism*, by a British "expert"—"expert" enclosed in quotation marks because the author himself, in line with the professional decorum of the day, confesses that "becoming a so-called expert on terrorism simply evolved from the fact that I spent such a lot of time talking about it." This is his view on human evolution:

> When *Homo erectus* [the species predating *Homo sapiens*, in the modern classification] first began competing with animals, not having their strength or claws he had to use his better brain to devise weapons, and to join his fellow-men in groups for their mutual protection. And the moment you have a group, you need a chief. And when you get sufficiently civilized to start cultivating the soil, and to think in terms of more than the moment, you need a hierarchy and a rule of law. And then to enforce that law your chief needs agents, and as soon as they appear on the scene there are bound to be others who are jealous of them and of the chief and want to overthrow their leaders. And there you are.

There you are. How naive this view is, not merely in the context of modern science, but also in the context of Plato's little myth, which tells us that respect and justice, not external authority and weapons, are what keep societies together. To approach terrorism, or any form of violence, from this expert's angle makes it difficult indeed to imagine a solution. In his myopic vision of what is achievable, the only visible protection from this menace is for those who can to spend more on "security" so that "instead of blowing up your plant they'll go down the road and blow up the next guy's plant." At least for now.

Why set up as an "expert" someone who, by his own admission, has so little to offer? Why, in the words of Erich Fromm, does the "*theory* of an innate aggressiveness [become] an *ideology* that helps . . . to rationalize the sense of impotence"? The best answer I have seen was written by a brilliant contemporary philosopher, Mary Midgley:

> The fact that people have survived so far shows only that they have the genetic equipment to meet the challenges they have so far encountered. Human pugnacity has its place in this equipment. But since people are now moving into a phase of existence when that pugnacity itself becomes one of the main dangers to be faced, new selective pressures are beginning to operate. In this situation telling people that they are *essentially* Chicago gangsters is not just false and confused, but mon-

strously irresponsible. . . . The unlucky thing is that people enjoy fatalism, partly because it promotes bad faith and excuse-making, partly because the melodrama has a sado-masochistic appeal—an appeal which gets stronger the nastier the powers [that control us] are supposed to be.

Fatalism appeals to those who do not wish to act. People like our British expert and so many others adopt the view that nature is ruthlessly deterministic *because* they do not wish to do anything about violence, not the other way around. The scientific truth is that nature includes no prescription for violence in human beings nor any mechanism for the working out of such a prescription if there were one.

This leads us to the disconcerting—but also liberating—conclusion that we are violent by some kind of choice. The question is, What kind? Certainly not conscious choice. The number of people who get up in the morning resolving to do at least one violent act before they get back to bed is surely small. We have already seen that the "decision" to sacrifice about 50,000 people annually to the automobile was not something we consciously debated as a culture. And—it is a truism that everybody wants peace, but nearly everybody does what leads to war.

The unconscious choices that lead us by more or less obscure pathways to violence rest on commitments we have already made and on unconscious assumptions about what life is and how to live it. It is difficult to change these commitments, but not impossible. We must try first of all to understand how and when we make them.

The poet W. H. Auden offers this observation:

When the human species is compared with other species, the most conspicuous difference is that . . . we seem to be born with no behavior-directing instincts; even the most elementary behavior required for physical survival and reproducing our kind has to be learned by each of us, either through imitation of or instruction by others. As Hazlitt said: "Without the aid of prejudice and custom I should not be able to find my way across the room."

Clearly the differences in people's "prejudices and customs" have a great bearing on the unconscious choices that can lead to violence. The city of Tokyo has an incidence of murder 400 times lower than its "sister city" of San Francisco. The 60 million inhabitants of Great Britain suffer fewer killings each year than the 1.5 million inhabitants of Manhattan who are ethnically similar to them.

The cultural determination that helps us get across the room—and that determines our readiness to turn to violence—is not nearly as absolute as the determination of "instincts" and genes. Viktor Frankl has brought out the poignancy of this fact:

> At the beginning of human history, man lost some of the basic animal instincts in which an animal's behavior is embedded and by which it is secured. Such security, like Paradise, is closed to man forever; man has to make choices. In addition to this, however ... the traditions that had buttressed his behavior are now rapidly diminishing. No instinct tells him what to do, and no tradition tells him what he ought to do; soon he will not know what he wants to do.

But we know what *we* want to do; we want to eliminate violence. And we can—by changing the elements of our culture that determine it. The decline of traditions has been working to our serious disadvantage insofar as the vacuum left by their guiding power has been filled by unenlightened, selfish interests such as advertising, entertainment, and the gun lobby that draw the forces of egotism and alienation into intense activity. But the same vacuum is an opportunity for those of us who want to reverse the process of alienation: Without the guiding hand of tradition, we can exert the more easily the power of our conscious choices on the elements of our culture that create dangerous unconscious attitudes. We are free to use that power to restore our culture's traditional ways of guiding people away from violence or to create new ones.

The suggestion that we tackle our own culture is not as iconoclastic as it seems (indeed others are "tackling" it already for much less healthy purposes), and it is certainly not a contradiction of nature. It is simply an expression of our uniquely human nature within the general design of evolution.

In the course of evolution, nature has not once but many times gone forward by quantum jumps. One instance, of course, was the multicellular organism itself (the first grand experiment in cooperation?). Another was the differentiation of specialized organ systems and then, among them, the central nervous system to coordinate the whole complex organism. The discovery and exploitation of the land environment was still another. And finally there came free choice. No animal has this. We may think with revulsion of a lion falling on a lamb, but not with outrage; yet if a man attacks a woman or any adult a child, outrage is just what we feel. When environmentalists speak of the slaughter of baby seals in Newfoundland or of elephants in Kenya, or when a child psychologist looks at what is fed to children on television, outrage is just what they feel. And their feeling is entirely appropriate because human beings are endowed with choice and thus with responsibility.

Each evolutionary leap produced a more dramatic form of life. Man is infinitely more stirring than the preceding orders of creation because of our infinite capacity to learn, to "create culture," as Lewin and Leakey have written, and to cooperate to such a degree that we have become "an animal with the potential to achieve virtually anything." And "the more we unravel the mysteries of brain and body function," a biologist adds,

> the more evident it becomes that we are built for moral evolution. . . . Man evolves when he uses his brain for unselfish rather than selfish aims. It means caring enough to have a strategy to meet the needs of neighbors across the street, across the border and across the world.

Thus nature herself puts in our hands the responsibility for continuing her handiwork of cooperation. In Auden's words, "a bee or an ant society endures in time from one generation to another automatically; a human society can only endure by conscious effort." Far from telling us we must act out the old impulses toward territoriality and aggression because we dare not "go against nature," science discovers that it *is* our nature to be responsive to higher guiding principles such as respect and justice, just as Plato said.

THE LESSON OF THE SIMPLE ONES

Quite a few societies exist in this world with much less violence than we do. Some are very much like our own—modern, industrialized states such as Sweden and Japan, which inhibit many forms of internal violence by regulating the availability of guns and by other common-sense measures. Yet they may show a high rate of suicide, get embroiled in international conflicts, or in other ways be as tangled in violence as we are.

Another small group of peaceable societies is in the modern world but not of it. These are religious communities such as the Hutterites on their farmsteads in the American Midwest, the Dukhovers who fled

Russia to work out their peaceful existence in Canada, and the Mennonites, some of whom have taken refuge in the upper reaches of the Amazon. These people, who practice voluntary simplicity and a degree of common ownership, who strive consciously to reward love and cooperation and to inhibit aggressiveness, are far freer from violence of all kinds than the parent societies from which they separated. They stay out of wars, have virtually no crime, and tend to lead long, useful, intentionally different lives, much less alienated than we are from one another, from themselves, and from their God.

Finally, there are a sizable number of technologically primitive communities that represent, as nearly as we can tell, life as it was lived by groups of *Homo sapiens* before the development of settled agriculture.

Recent archeological discoveries have shown that this way of life, too, was often far more peaceful than our own. At an important site called Koster in the lower Illinois valley, the early Indians apparently "came and went ... over a span of more than nine thousand years without any sign of cataclysm or replacement of local inhabitants through annihilation." This first site on the American continent where a record of such continuous habitation could be found bears witness to a simple gathering-and-hunting existence unmarred by violent calamity for 500 generations.

Even the new economy of settled agriculture, which is often cited as a precursor of war, did not always lead to war. For literally thousands of years, physically modern peoples inhabited the steppes of Europe and western Asia in stable and (by later standards) small agricultural communities. These "Old European" peoples were matrilineal, it seems, and lived in egalitarian communities without furnishing elaborate burials for a royal or military elite: In fact, their houses and lands have not yielded one artifact that has to be classified as a weapon, though there are examples of hauntingly beautiful pottery and other manufactures. We find no sign of a defensive wall around the settlements. It was not until the fifth millennium B.C. that these peoples began to be gradually overrun by successive waves of Kurgan (barrow) peoples who had domesticated the horse and were pushing westward in search of pastures and living space for their growing populations. It is thought that these newcomers were our cultural ancestors, the Indo-Europeans:

> The Old European and Kurgan cultures were the antithesis of one
> another. One economy based on farming, the other on stock breeding
> and grazing, produced two contrasting ideologies. The Old European
> belief system focused on the agricultural cycle of birth, death, and
> regeneration, embodied in the feminine principle, a Mother Creatrix.
> The Kurgan ideology ... exalted virile, heroic warrior gods of the
> shining and thunderous sky. Weapons are nonexistent in Old European
> imagery; whereas the dagger and battle-axe are dominant symbols of the
> Kurgans, who like all historically known Indo-Europeans, glorified the
> lethal power of the sharp blade.

In the course of 3,000 to 4,000 years the new arrivals relentlessly
imposed their "virile" ideology throughout this vast territory by conquest or cultural assimilation—even as they were to do millennia later in
North America. Yet in other parts of the world, a number of peaceable communities have survived to modern times, enabling us to form
a better impression of their earlier life than we could from the archeological record alone.

One day in 1966 a Philippine hunter named Dafal was traversing the
island of Mindanao and found himself face to face with the Stone Age.
He had stumbled upon the Tasaday, a now much-studied band of
thirteen adults and thirteen children. No one knows how long the
Tasaday had lived there, sheltered from history in the crater of an extinct
volcano. Almost everyone who has visited the Tasaday since has been
impressed with their remarkable gentleness and affection. John Nance,
author of *The Gentle Tasaday*, found them to be "inspiring emblems of
social peace and harmony, of, simply, love. Their love was everywhere—for each other, for their forest, for us—for life."

Are the Tasaday born that way? Many anthropologists observed that
Tasaday children are like kids anywhere in the world. They squabble,
fight over a stick, make striking gestures at one another. But by the time
they are adults this "normal" aggressiveness is no more—outgrown. The
secret is that by their traditional educational system the Tasaday "discourage aggressive behavior, reward cooperative behavior, and set models in themselves for their children to imitate." These words are worth
taking to heart.

Many other simple (or, if you will, primitive) cultures maintain such
responsible standards for intragroup relationships. Some, such as the
Tasaday, the Arapesh of New Guinea, the Lepchas of Sikkim, the

Mbuti Pygmies, and the Semai of Malaya seem to thrive with no violence at all. Others—the Eskimo, the Punan of Borneo, the Hadza of Tanzania, the !Kung Bushmen of the Kalahari Desert, the Baiga, Toda, and Birhor of South India, the Polynesian Ifaluk, the Lapps, and several American Indian groups—live with very little. In all of them, in contrast to other nonliterate societies that are not especially peaceable, the formula is the same: They reward cooperation and discourage aggression. That is their culture.

Once while she was studying an Eskimo community an anthropologist blew up at another European who had carelessly destroyed an Eskimo canoe. She was quite taken aback when the whole village gave her the cold shoulder for several weeks. A canoe is a precious article in the precarious existence of those people, but what she had threatened with her outburst was more precious still. As a Bushman who had witnessed a similar loss of temper in a European said, "If you want to help people, don't get angry with them. Keep calm."

There must be more to nonviolent culture than avoiding conflict and anger. The !Kung, for example, are a highly sociable people who spend a great deal of time visiting and talking over the business of the community—who will hunt with whom, when should they move to the next watering place, is it time for a subgroup to depart. But in addition to work, which is not too arduous for the !Kung, they spend a good deal of time in partly ritualized games and dances. In their games, significantly, "competitiveness . . . is almost entirely lacking, and the players appear to come into a game for the sheer joy of it and for practicing their own skill at it."

If people can live and play like this, can it be necessary for human beings to express aggressive drives as such, especially when culture provides prosocial channels for these drives? The facts that such people thrive in environments ranging from the steaming jungles of Borneo to the frozen tundras of the Arctic Circle and that their nonviolence works in societies as small as the single Tasaday clan or in spread-out and constantly regrouping communities like the !Kung show that the ability to socialize aggression does not depend on climate or ease of living or group size any more than it depends on heredity. It is determined by choice and preserved by an ongoing interaction of culture and individual effort.

The evidence of evolution is clear: A state of zero violence is humanly possible. In the next chapter we will hear the testimony of history; but first let us pause to see what else we may have already gained.

When Westerners first came into contact with them, the Maori of New Zealand were not among the world's most nonviolent societies. Yet in the course of their cultural evolution, they had evolved a system of conflict regulation that required all-out war to be preceded by a long series of ritualized escalating combats consisting of feints and dodges in which nobody got hurt, except perhaps in his pride. Not many people were hurt in the rare wars that did result, either, as their primitive implements were not very efficient. Revenge was not a problem, because Maori ideology allowed for the swallowing of losses and for some military defeats.

This situation remained stable and satisfactory, if less than perfect, for centuries. Then the European traders and whaling crews introduced muskets. Maori groups living close to the trading ports were the first to acquire the new weapons and turn them against other groups, who "had no choice" but to respond in kind. Fighting for revenge became both more frequent and much more lethal throughout New Zealand. It has been estimated that in just two decades tens of thousands of Maoris, or between one-quarter and one-half of the total Maori population of New Zealand, perished—some in battle, others because of starvation and disease resulting from the neglect of subsistence labors while warfare and arms races were going on, forcing the people to produce goods that could be traded to Europeans for guns and ammunition.

What finally saved the Maori from extinction, interestingly enough, was that many of them became Christians and abandoned the institution of fighting for revenge; finally they abandoned fighting with muskets among themselves. What the equivalent of Christianity would be among modern civilizations that already think they "have" it, is not clear. What *is* clear is that the modern world is undergoing problems with very similar dynamics on a larger scale. What European traders did to the Maori—introducing potent weapons their social systems could not accommodate—is what the United States, the Soviet Union, and other industrialized powers are doing all over the Third World today. What the Maori groups did to one another—cause conflicts and the use of weapons to escalate—is exactly what both developed and developing nations are doing among themselves.

To understand this pattern, it may help to look farther back into nature through one of Konrad Lorenz's discoveries, since confirmed by other ethologists and anthropologists. Lorenz found that the capability of animals of a given species to deal with their own aggression can be tested by putting them into extreme circumstances, such as crowded cages in which basic resources such as food and water are limited. Under pressure of this kind, he discovered, most of the dangerous predators like lions and tigers survived fairly well. With the usual roaring and bluffing and threatening one another into submission, they quickly sorted themselves into peaceful social hierarchies. It was the timid animals, the very symbols of passivity like the rabbits and the doves, who killed one another off. With whatever "defensive" equipment they had, strange to say, they would gnaw and peck one another to death.

But this makes perfect sense. Predators have very destructive physical equipment and the dispositions to go with it, but they also cannot afford to lie around nursing wounds; they have to be fit to hunt. Most of them have to cooperate to bring down their prey, so they had to learn either not to fight with one another or to fight in such a way, as another animal behaviorist has said, that "contestants rarely get injured, [which] is in the best interests of both winner and loser." An animal that does not have very destructive equipment to begin with has not had the same need to develop social habits to deal with its own aggression.

We might look upon humanity today as a basically nonviolent species that finds itself in a limited, overcrowded facility. The human animal, like the early primates, is physically not a predator. But we have used our miraculous learning abilities to go far beyond our biological equipment in gaining access to destructive force. Especially the technological advances of the last 200 years have upset the balance between power and control so seriously as to bring us to the brink of annihilation. Suddenly we have "teeth" like a lion but the undeveloped social instincts of a rabbit—and we're in a very overcrowded cage.

Must we then go "back to nature" in some way? That could not possibly work. In a primitive community, if the primary mechanisms for conflict resolution fail, one of the parties can often just pack up and leave. "In the face of something displeasing," anthropologist Peggy Durdin reported, the Tasaday "seem to use the tactic of evasion: they simply walk away." As effective a final recourse as this may be, it belongs to their world, not ours. Theirs was the world of free-ranging gatherer-hunters, when the number of *Homo sapiens* on the globe was on the order of 10 million. Ours is a world of 4,000 million, about two-thirds of whom are starving and about one-third of whom have or are seeking the ability to deliver death to millions anywhere on the planet in thirty minutes. What we need is not evasion, separation, but cooperation. Unity.

In June of 1979 a man named John Spenkelink was executed at the Florida State Prison at Raiford. The case received nationwide attention because he was the first person executed under the reinstated penalty, which Florida had let fall into abeyance some years before, and so his last words reached many people: "Man is what he chooses to be. He chooses that for himself." *Time* called this an "enigmatic" remark, but there was nothing enigmatic about it. Men and women surely choose their destinies, both as individuals and groups.

And what destiny shall we now choose? From the era of the cave-sheltering family the circle with which a human being had to learn to cooperate has steadily grown, passing the level of the seminomadic band of about forty souls (like the Tasaday), the multifamily settlement, and the city-state to the modern nation. Where shall we go from here? Not "back to nature" in the romantic sense, but surely back to the path that nature launched us on, the way of evolution from individuality to unity. Otherwise our destructive power will turn our closeness and enhanced interdependency into a horrible setback for all life. Our only choice, if you can call it a choice, is to tear the world apart or else make it our own—to make all of it, for each of us, the final circle.

5|Forgotten History

The spirit of this country is totally adverse to a large military force.

Thomas Jefferson (1807)

I want to stand by my country, but I cannot vote for war. I say no.

Jeanette Rankin (1917)

Scientists "observe nature," but what they see is deeply colored by what they believe. As a result, they describe a world with specific if unseen horizons until a Galileo or an Einstein or a Heisenberg comes along to show that there is much more in nature than these narrow horizons hold. Historians too—as well as the rest of us—see very much what they are predisposed to see, with the same profound implications for what they—and we—believe is possible. What gives value to a human life, as Wordsworth put it, are the "little, nameless, unremembered acts / Of kindness and of love." Yet as with evolution, so with history: The acts of violence are what are remembered. Somehow only what is negative seems real. This bias, to quote Mary Midgley, "has two great attractions, both of which it shares with Hedonism—its great apparent simplifying effect, and its swashbuckling style."

If you want to see this distortion taking shape before your eyes, look at history in the making, namely, that peculiar modern slant on what is real that we call news. Some months after the Soviets invaded Afghanistan—June 9, 1980, to be exact—the Soviet press reported an astounding breakthrough. Soviet leader Brezhnev met with India's Foreign Minister P. V. N. Rao and said, "The Soviet Union wants a political settlement on Afghanistan." Here was a signal for peace, but who in this country saw it? The news was carried in a three-inch-long article that appeared on page 46 of the *San Francisco Chronicle* for that day, under a headline that does not even hint at its importance: "Brezhnev Hosts

India Diplomat." (The front pages were full of "news" about sex spas in San Francisco.)

At the time the American government was preparing us psychologically and militarily for the "inevitable" outcome of the "crisis" in Afghanistan: war between the superpowers, with nuclear arms not ruled out. However, if an American president were to catch the significance of an event like this, he could be on the phone to Mr. Brezhnev in half an hour and say, "I'm for it! Let's get together and negotiate a political settlement right away." It could lead to the resolution not only of the Afghan crisis but of the crisis of military tensions throughout the world. I, for one, find this a "swashbuckling" idea. But as long as we read in the newspapers full reports of how many Soviets and Afghans are killing one another while all signs of hope are systematically buried in the back pages—or in newsroom wastebaskets—we are simplifying our view of the world by closing the door to our most important options.

This incident suggests the difficulty with what we regard as history. Professional historians are much too sophisticated to believe what they read in popular sources such as newspapers, but historians are human, and cannot easily escape the besetting biases of the human outlook. History does not have to be "exciting" the way modern news media do, but it is nonetheless surrounded by strong magnetic fields that compromise its objectivity.

Tolstoy draws our attention to the preface of a history textbook, then in its twenty-sixth edition, which was standard in all the secondary schools in France. The author of the text, a certain M. Lavisse, defines unembarrassedly *why* French boys are taught history: The Germans took away Alsace and Lorraine, the French "have always avenged their fathers"; so we teach you this history "*to make good soldiers out of you.*" This kind of history—so-called—is not a science. It is not an attempt to discover the truth or to find out the possibilities of the future; it is a commitment to perpetuate errors of the past.

No historian would write a preface like that today. But few historians can escape the pervasive pessimism of our age. From evolutionary sciences, from archeology, from anthropology and animal behavior, we have just been seeing evidence that war is recent, unnecessary, and sporadic. Yet Richard Coudenhove-Kalergi can generalize that the "stuff of history is war," adding significantly, "and indeed the natural state of human society is war."

It is as though we were sitting outside the house in which a family is living out its life. The family might draw closer to one another, talk, sometimes argue, write books, play music, all the "little, nameless, unremembered acts / Of kindness and of love" that we outside would never hear. Yet if a violent fight happened to break out, we would suddenly hear the shouting and perhaps the crash of breaking objects.

Isn't this the way that history observes and preserves events? Suppose I want to write a history of the century and a half of unbroken peace that Sweden recently celebrated. If I write about August Strindberg, Carl Larsson, Gustaf Fröding, that will be intellectual history. If I write about people such as Nobel, that will be history of science or industrial history. I could do something called economic or cultural history. But if I want to write something that, starting from Herodotus and Thucydides, we have come to regard as just plain history, I will have a hard time doing so because the "history" of Sweden's last 170 years (her last war was with Finland in 1809) has been "uneventful." Maybe the Swedish experience holds more valuable lessons for humankind than the history of Europe from 1939 to 1945, but it would have a hard time competing for attention against the dramatic, destructive events of that latter period. It was Gandhi—who was no historian but who had a sense of history many historians might envy—who finally put it best: History as we know it studies *breakdowns* in the world process, it "records only the interruptions in the even development of *ahimsa*"—cooperation, unity, love.

If we are serious about wanting to know what light history can shed on our question, whether zero violence is possible, we have to look at some of history's neglected episodes that clearly show the "impossible" to have happened, and right here. It is a necessary corrective. Not long ago a student of mine said, "I'd like to take your course on nonviolence, Mr. Nagler, but . . . I read history." I only wish he did.

AMERICA REVISED

Few people stop to think that the expression "Quaker State" once designated much more than a particular brand of motor oil. In 1681 the vast, fertile colony of what is now Pennsylvania was deeded to William Penn by the British crown. Penn dreamed of setting up a colony in the Americas where people not only of his own religious persuasion, the

Quakers, but also of all persuasions could come to escape persecution and build a life based on religious principles and values. Penn was one of the most remarkable men of his time. The son of a famous admiral (after whom the colony was named; Penn wanted it simply called Sylvania), he had distinguished himself in military exploits while defending his father's territories in Ireland. But in his early years he had also had some religious experiences, and by the 1680s he had already come under the influence of the rapidly growing Religious Society of Friends (the Quakers). The Friends must have understood his spiritual experiences much better than members of the established churches did, and in due time Penn became a close associate and biographer of the remarkable founder of the movement, George Fox.

It is very difficult to describe Fox in a few words. After an early boyhood mystical experience in which, as he said, "I came to know the hidden unity in the Eternal Being," he became a complete nonconformist and from there an uncompromising reformer. "Unity with the creation" was a favorite phrase. Summing up his impression of George Fox years later, Penn related that "in all things he acquitted himself like a man, yea, a strong man, a new and heavenly-minded man; a divine and a naturalist, and all of God Almighty's making." Fox had once so impressed a band of soldiers who were detailed to guard him that instead of returning him to the verminous seventeenth-century dungeon he was imprisoned in, they offered him the "preferment" of being their captain. But Fox told them, "I knew whence all wars arose, even from the lusts, according to James' doctrine; and . . . I lived in the virtue of that life and power that took away the occasion of all wars." Fox was promptly sent back to Derby Gaol for six more months, but his retort became the basis of the famous "Quaker peace testimony," which for 300 years has encouraged thousands of men and women to live in the way that "takes away the occasion" of violence.

Fox himself was the greatest exemplar of this life. Despite howls of protest, he never stopped his spontaneous preaching—from haystacks (it was against his principles to use an established "steeple house"), on shipboard, from the prisoner's dock of rural assizes, even trotting alongside Oliver Cromwell's carriage. Time after time, after standing undaunted by the uproar or by physical threats, "the power and the seed of the Lord God" manifest in his presence, he would still the mob, and new Friends would come forward to bear witness to the power of nonviolence. Throughout the British Isles, Holland, France, Germany, the Carolinas, and the wilds of North America Fox took this message with his inexhaustible enthusiasm.

William Penn brought this "seed" to his new seat of government in Pennsylvania. The result was what we call today the Holy Experiment, for some seventy years a beacon of simplicity and enlightened governance based not on the power to coerce but on respect.

Penn's first step was to treat the Delaware Indians, into whose territory destiny had brought him, on a basis of absolute equality. His first letter to them, sent in 1683 before his arrival in the colony, was a century ahead of its time in its testimony to racial equality. He spoke of the God who was their common father and had written his law of kindness in their hearts, and said:

> Now this great God hath been pleased to make me concerned in your parts of the world, and the king of the country where I live hath given unto me a great province, but I desire to enjoy it with your love and consent, that we may always live together as neighbors and friends; else what would the great God say to us, who hath made us not to devour and destroy one another, but to live soberly and kindly together in the world? Now I would have you well observe, that I am very sensible of the unkindness and injustice that hath been too much exercised toward you by the people of these parts of the world, who sought themselves, and to make great advantages by you, rather than be examples of justice and goodness unto you.... But I am not such a man, as is well known in my own country; I have great love and regard toward you, and I desire to win and gain your love and friendship, by a kind, just and peaceable life, and the people I send are of the same mind.

Penn proved as good as his word. Any Indian brought to trial in Pennsylvania, for example, was guaranteed a half-Indian jury. As a result, while Indian wars were raging in the other colonies, leaving a residue of bitterness that has not been resolved to this day, Pennsylvania was an oasis of peace as long as his principles were observed.

In civil law, the experiment was no less remarkable. Only twelve crimes were punishable by hanging, during a period when the English criminal code listed over two hundred. Anticipating an enlightenment that has still not fully dawned, "Penn dared to replace revenge with reform," as Quaker historians say, and instead of isolating or simply punishing criminals, decreed that "all prisons shall be workhouses ... whereof one shall be in every county." No other colony was such a successful melting pot. It held Germans, Swedes, Dutch, English, Welsh, Irish, and others of every religious persuasion of the time. Further, Penn almost succeeded in preventing the importation of black slaves (in those days even the Friends weren't ready to go that far with him) and did succeed for a long time in protecting the colony from external invasions without a militia.

The seventeenth century in Europe had seen the birth of an idea: that man can live without war. As a concept in international law, this idea had been promulgated by early jurists such as Vattel, Pufendorf, and the great Grotius in Holland, while humanistic philosophers and religious thinkers in the new spirit of the Reformation dreamed of a community of nations living under treaties of "perpetual peace." To this tradition Penn contributed his *Essay Towards the Present and Future Peace of Europe* in 1692, drawing upon his successful experiments with disarmament in America. The essay has never ranked with those of Dante, Erasmus, Rousseau, or Kant or caused as much trouble. But ideas are one thing. Here was a ruler not only taking up the pen but laying down the sword. More than two centuries before the League of Nations, he was trying to put these ideas into practice.

Most Pennsylvanians then, as would most of us now, lacked a frame of reference to understand what Penn was doing. They, and even more so the anxious imperialists watching from across the Atlantic, failed to connect the colony's security with its nonviolent—or at least un-armed—state. So arose the paradox that Penn's greatest and potentially most valuable success stirred up the greatest panic. Being so far ahead of his time, and being hampered by British imperial policy, in which Pennsylvania was enmeshed as a colony of the British crown, Penn had to defend his vision against heavy attacks. Yet the defense was so successful that the Quaker element was still holding its ground about a generation after Penn's death in 1718. Then, shortly before statehood and American independence, the Quakers were outvoted and resigned from the government. "Quaker State" was on its way to meaning a brand of motor oil.

The most important lesson in this episode, and one that will be repeated in the episodes to follow, is that as long as Pennsylvania as a whole clung more or less to nonviolent principles the movement never failed in open contest with an external power. Pennsylvania was not overrun by the French or the Hessians, least of all by the Delaware

Indians. If we may anticipate, historian Judith Brown has pointed out that more than two centuries later in the greatest nonviolent struggle of all time "internal strains . . . weakened each all-India *satyāgraha* [nonviolent campaign], sometimes destroying them with eruptions of violence directed not only or even mainly at the British but against other Indians." Likewise in Pennsylvania nonviolence held against external foes until at length, due to internal dissensions, the light within the colony itself sputtered and grew dim.

Even with this failure, the "friendly seed" that Fox had transplanted to the colonies did not die out. Our constitutional guarantee of freedom of conscience, written in as the first article of the Bill of Rights, was based on the legislation of Penn and the Quaker government of Rhode Island. Furthermore, the influence of the Friends and other peace sects of the time was hardly limited to those who sat in the seats of power such as Isaac Penington, Judge Fell, Penn, or Roger Williams. There was the unseen influence of the martyrs of the tempestuous early period, women and men such as Mary Dyer (hanged on Boston Common, 1660), and the phenomenon of John Woolman. Before the Holy Experiment quite came apart in Pennsylvania Woolman, a simple tailor with a "tender conscience," was walking the length and breadth of the Eastern Seaboard, speaking out at Friends' meetings and to anyone else he could reach, red, white, or black. Along with simple living and nonviolence, Woolman made the unification of all races a part of his central commitment. Almost a century earlier, in 1688, the Germantown Friends had renounced slaveholding when they themselves came to these shores to escape prison and persecution: "There is a liberty of conscience here," they said, "which is right and reasonable, and there ought to be likewise liberty of the body." Keeping to this tradition, Woolman wrote in 1746, "To consider mankind otherwise than brethren, to think favors are peculiar to one nation and exclude others, plainly supposes a darkness in the understanding."

By speaking in this vein, and much more by backing up his words with his personal demeanor and his own renunciation, Woolman convinced many Friends and others not to hold slaves. What is even more remarkable (but typical of the Friends), he also advocated justice for slaveholders and put the same energy into advocating that they be compensated when giving up their slaves involved an unusual hardship, as in the South if often did. If the later abolition movement had cherished this equality of vision, the bitterness and destruction wrought by the Civil War—indeed the war itself, one of the bloodiest in history—might have been avoided. It might equally have been avoided if enough slaveholders had listened. As the great historian G. M. Trevelyan has said, "Close your ears to John Woolman one century, and you will get John Brown the next, with Grant to follow." And, Quaker historian Tolles adds, "bitter legacies of hatred persisting still, a century after."

In the colonial era nonviolence was not confined to Quakers. As tensions built toward the Revolutionary War there was also a strong nonviolent momentum. We see it in the Suffolk Resolves, passed by the delegates of Suffolk County, Massachusetts Bay, in 1774:

> We would heartily recommend to all persons of this community not to engage in any routs, riots or licentious attacks upon the properties of any persons whatsoever, as being subversive of all order and government; but, by a steady, manly, uniform, and persevering opposition, to convince our enemies that in a contest so important—in a cause so solemn, our conduct shall be such as to merit the approbation of the wise, and the admiration of the brave and free of every age and of every country.

At least one scholar, Gene Sharp (from whom I take the phrase "forgotten history"), argues that independence would have come sooner if this momentum had prevailed and there had been no war at all.

According to a certain view of history, the Holy Experiment and the nonviolent momentum that preceded the War of Independence failed to reach their goals. But they will not have failed completely as long as some can grasp their significance. For example, looking back on the Holy Experiment in the nineteenth century the influential Quaker Jonathan Dymond wrote that the "only natural opportunity which the virtue of the Christian world has afforded us of ascertaining the safety of relying upon God for defense, has determined that it is safe."

Staughton Lynd, Charles Chatfield, and other modern historians have shown that the search for a more unifying and less conformist direction for this country continues this side of Independence too—a tradition constantly surfacing in little people, little groups, little movements, focused on the same social issues of ethnic equality, penal reform, and international peace.

Adin Ballou might serve as a typical nineteenth-century example. In 1842 he founded a utopian community at Hopedale, Massachusetts, which lasted some fourteen years, until two brothers who owned most of its stock withdrew. Ballou's *Christian Non-Resistance*, though dated in style and hardly read today, sets out forcefully that "non-injurious force" or love can be harnessed and put to work in daily action and that Christ was as serious as he was practical in exhorting us to "resist not evil" by evil but in the words of Paul, to "overcome evil with good." Ballou was a vigorous opponent of slavery (he knew William Lloyd Garrison and the other prominent abolitionists) and wrote with passion, and surprising foresight, about women's rights and subjects like penal reform: "Reliance on injurious penal force costs more than it comes to . . . If no more than what is expended in detecting, trying, and punishing criminals, were judiciously applied to work of prevention and reformation it would accomplish ten times more for society." But his major concern was peace. At various times an active speaker and writer with the American Peace Society, whose founding in 1828 made it one of the earliest of such organizations in this country, Ballou was one of the few abolitionists, perhaps the only prominent one, to keep faith with pacifism in the face of the Civil War.

The Civil War was a shattering interruption of the peace process in America. Nothing is more confounding for an idealistic movement that is not yet mature and self-possessed than the prospect of a holy war. Many idealistic abolitionists were seduced by the age-old temptation to use wrong means to bring about right ends. In effect, they sacrificed their highest ideal, peace, to purchase abolition, and ended up with neither. Of course, the Civil War seemed effective to those who did not look too deeply or were not gifted with our hindsight. How were they to know that well after 100 years there would still be bitterness between North and South and that blacks in the United States would be free only on paper—until this century, when they found the more potent weapon of nonviolence. Much later, visionaries as unknown as Ernest Howard Crosby ("If the South Had Been Allowed to Go," 1903) and as well known as John Kenneth Galbraith could say that abolition was *delayed* by the Civil War or would have come without it. In those days, who could know this but Ballou, Burritt, and a few others on the visionary fringe?

The United States entered the second half of the nineteenth century with its peace movements badly disorganized, ill prepared for the American expansionism that began at the end of that century or for our impending involvement in two world wars. Yet scattered as they were, the sparks had not died out. One such spark ignited the arbitration movement, an ancestor of the current concepts of conciliation and mediation. In 1874 both houses of Congress passed a resolution that an arbitration clause should be included in all United States treaties; a stronger version was passed in the 1890s. Both were ignored by the State Department. The National Arbitration League (1882), the Christian Arbitration Association (1886), and the Lake Mohawk Arbitration Conferences (1895–1916) kept plugging away, giving rise to a number of organizations and efforts that are still with us. This activity paralleled the movement across the Atlantic, called liberal internationalism, an attempt to breathe life into the idea of the Duc de Sully and Abbé de St. Pierre and William Penn that the nations of Europe should confederate before it was too late. Like that earlier movement, internationalism was severely interrupted by a cataclysmic war—in August, 1914; but it has never died.

Another spark was pacifism, the individual man's or woman's refusal to cooperate in war. There were about 4,000 conscientious objectors in this country during World War I and 16,000 in Britain (not counting the rebellious Irish). These numbers waxed and waned in the confusions of our century, but the concept of conscientious objection to warfare has become steadily more legitimate. At the time of this writing, a consortium of peace groups is working to put on the UN agenda the proposal that conscientious objection should be recognized as a universal human right.

Numbers are not necessarily all-important in something like pacifism: As Einstein once said, if 5 percent of the people would work for peace, peace would prevail. Setting aside those who object only to a particular war, even one woman or man willing to suffer or die as a living example (what is sometimes called a moral witness) of the truth that life is not expendable can be a tremendous force that cannot but awaken human conscience in the long run. As Trevelyan said, governments ignore this kind of witness at their peril.

Yet they do ignore it. And the gap between vision and effectiveness—at least the kind of effectiveness that history acknowledges—remained wide well into our century. By and large, it still seemed that one was either idealistically pure but socially ineffectual (like Ballou) or else succumbed to the temptation to use violence and was immediately effective, but only at creating havoc (like Garrison). Gandhi was what was needed to bring action and idea together. Keenly appreciated by a responsive handful in this country, Gandhi catalyzed the most successful experiment in social progress America has ever seen, by enabling a young divinity student, Martin Luther King, Jr., to make a great ideal into a social force:

> Gandhi was probably the first person in history to lift the love ethic of Jesus above mere interaction between individuals to a powerful and effective social force on a large scale.... It was in this Gandhian emphasis on love and nonviolence that I discovered the method for social reform that I had been seeking for so many months.

Does history show that war and violence are inevitable? I believe it shows instead that our desire for peace is unquenchable but that we will never fulfill that desire until we place it above all other desires and, further, that there has never been a better time or place to take this final step toward peace than here and now.

Throughout the recent, continuing tragedy in Nicaragua, no one seems to have remembered that in 1926 a fearless Quaker pacifist named John Nevin Sayre rode into the Nicaraguan jungles to mediate between the insurgent general Sandino (from whom the present Sandinistas took their name) and his enemies, which included the U.S. Marines. Had the Marine Corps commander but let Sayre through, he might have spared that country all the blood that has spilled there, then and now. A great historian giving a balanced view of our country would tell of many deeds like this. Such a history would be studded with names such as Sojourner Truth, Elihu Burritt, Lucretia Mott, A. J. Muste, Jeanette Rankin, Kirby Page, Jane Addams—not the names of people who built railroads but of people who built a braver concept of humanity. It would record their words, like the fiery sermons Page delivered against war, the "most colossal social sin." It would not allow them to be omitted from our heritage.

A NOTABLE COMPARISON, RARELY NOTED

I am constantly reminded of a cartoon that showed a prisoner staring wistfully through the bars of his cell at the flowers and trees and sunshine and people outside, not realizing that the cell had no back wall.

We could walk out of the violence trap at any time if we only realized that it is possible to do so, if we could learn to turn around.

Albert Szent-Györgyi, a Nobel laureate in medicine, is one of the few men who seems to have seen the missing wall of our cell in the twentieth century. In the years preceding World War II, Szent-Györgyi repeatedly escaped the Gestapo by the skin of his teeth. He is not a romantic; he knows what violence is about. He writes:

> Between the two world wars, at the heyday of colonialism, force reigned supreme. It had a suggestive power, and it was natural for the weaker to lie down before the stronger.
>
> Then came Gandhi, chasing out of his country, almost single-handed, the greatest military power on earth. He taught the world that there are higher things than force, higher even than life itself; he proved that force had lost its suggestive power.

If Szent-Györgyi is right, this demonstration is one of the greatest advances in human history, perhaps in human evolution. The world will never be the same. The reason no one realizes what has happened is that it takes time for a breakthrough so simple and so enormous to create in people's minds the fact of its own possibility. Most of us in the West do not even know the facts of what Gandhi did in India, much less appreciate what they portend. How could we? In a world where hostility is taken for granted as the only relationship between parties with a conflict of separate interest, where our newspapers, our histories, our very world view do not even dream of a force other than coercive power, how can we assimilate such an event? Szent-Györgyi, Einstein, William Shirer, and a few others have understood; the rest of us have not.

In my experience, people reflexively raise two objections to the claim that Gandhi's accomplishments in India are epochal. One is that Gandhi and his nonviolence had nothing to do with India's independence; Britain was ruined by the world wars and could not afford to keep her empire. Even if this were true, would it be relevant? Anyone who has seen the remarkable newsreels of the British finally leaving India after two centuries of exploitation, their soldiers cheered by the Indian people, can see that Gandhi's political achievement was not independence but independence realized *cooperatively*, raising both oppressor and oppressed into a closer relationship of friendship and respect.

The other, and more common, objection is that nonviolence would only work against people like the British, with their notorious sense of fair play and decency (a sensibility perhaps not so highly rated among beneficiaries of the "white man's burden" in Kenya, Rhodesia, Burma—and India). "It would never have worked against the Nazis," people typically respond. I usually suggest to proponents of this view that they look at a few reels of news from the Indian struggle for independence; review the history of attacks on civilians, hangings, floggings, mass imprisonments, and humiliations; or read the eyewitness accounts of correspondents such as Webb Miller, who described the brutal treatment nonviolent resisters received. When the British *raj* met with resistance it reacted with the same violence in India—not to mention Kenya—that has characterized imperial behavior all over the world. The British mentality in India differed, but only in degree from that of other European colonials in Asia and Africa. By and large, their attitude was as one of E. M. Forster's characters epitomized it somewhere in *A Passage to India*: "We have come here to rule this country by force."

And, interestingly enough, nonviolence *did* work against the Nazis. Consider the example of the Norwegian schoolteachers' strike, which began during the German occupation in the spring of 1942 and was partly inspired by a man named Haaken Holmboe, who had some acquaintance with Gandhi's work. The Quisling regime had drawn up a master plan to convert the entire educational system of Norway to the service of indoctrinating Nazi values, threatening to dismiss any teacher who did not comply. More than 90 percent of the teachers refused. Despite all kinds of harassment, they did not give in. Finally they were deported to concentration camps above the Arctic Circle, where they were forced to do hard labor on starvation rations, but they did not give in. The Gestapo circulated a rumor that they were going to shoot every tenth man, hoping that their wives would persuade them to capitulate; but even this backfired. Mrs. Holmboe, whose husband was in the concentration camp, came to one of the teachers who was inclined to yield and told him, "We women do not wish you to yield. We are prepared to run the risk," and the teachers did not give in. The Gestapo gave in. They brought the teachers back to Oslo, where they assembled to hear Quisling sputtering at them, "You teachers, you have ruined everything for me!"

Another success was even more instructive. It took place in the heart of Berlin, 1943, when the day came for the arrest of every Jew living in Germany. All day long the trucks guarded by armed SS troops rolled through the streets while passers-by looked away. A special prison in the Rosenstrasse had been set aside for Jews "with Aryan kin"—mostly men with non-Jewish wives—where they were concentrated like the others, not knowing what was in store for them.

The following morning, as if summoned by some mysterious command, the wives of these men began to gather at the gates of the Rosenstrasse detention center, calling for the release of their husbands. Security police tried again and again to disperse them, but they only grew in number and determination while their husbands, against strict orders, crowded to the windows and cried out for release. Gestapo headquarters was only a few blocks away; Gestapo leaders, fanatical, iron-willed, had only to order a few minutes of machine-gun fire to eliminate the disturbance, but somehow they didn't. They agreed to negotiate with the women and, finally, released their husbands. Some Jews in this category survived the entire holocaust because their wives stood by them through twelve years of inhuman persecution.

The wives' demonstration was completely unplanned and disorganized, and it fell apart just as spontaneously after its initial success. The Norwegian strike succeeded further because it persisted further, just as nonviolence succeeded in India where it persisted but did not succeed, say, in South Africa in the 1950s, where Chief Albert Luthuli's nonviolent resistance effort broke down in the face of the Sharpeville massacre. Courage, especially sustained courage, infallibly evokes respect. Most white Southerners had scant respect for black people in the 1960s; but when they saw blacks under King's leadership bearing threats and suffering without backing down, many grew to respect them, though not all had the courage to admit it.

Whether organized nonviolent resistance by Jews would have "worked" in Nazi Germany, that is, whether it would have substantially mitigated or halted their nearly unchecked extermination, cannot be proved from history because it was never tried—not in Germany, not in Poland, not in Hungary, not in the Soviet Union. The degree to which individuals tried to deal with Nazis nonviolently, as opposed to passively, is largely unrecorded.

Yet history does record literally thousands of cases in which groups or nations have successfully coped with armed aggression without recourse to violence. Gene Sharp, for example, has categorized and discussed well over two hundred in his *Politics of Non-Violent Action*, a book that should be far better known. Most of these cases stop far short of being active nonviolence as it was understood by Gandhi and King (which I'll say more about in a later chapter). They were mostly slapdash, spur-of-the-moment affairs carried out by people who did not have the option of armed resistance and adopted some sort of nonviolence by default, like the wives of the Jewish prisoners in 1943. Elihu Burritt, for example, cites the successful resistance of the Sandwich Islanders against a French gunboat that had landed marines to "punish" the little native monarchy for levying a tax on French brandy and wine. Rather than try to man their broken-down stockade, the king told his people to carry on their business as usual and politely ignore the raiders. The heavily armed marines felt so silly that after venting their fury on the empty stockade they just sailed away. Burritt writes:

> The full power revealed and prescribed in that simple and sublime precept of the Gospel, "overcome evil with good," has never been tested by any people, population, or community.... To put it into full operation, requires a capacity of good-will, of forgiveness of injuries, of abnegation of natural instincts, which the population of no town, or province, or state, has ever acquired. But ... a case has occurred here and there, in which a considerable community has acquired the ability of sustaining for awhile the lowest, feeblest, manifestation of this power, or a condition of *passive resistance* to oppression armed with a force which could instantly crush any violent opposition they might attempt to array against it.

To this day, as activist and writer David Dellinger has pointed out, the "theory and practice of active nonviolence are roughly at the [same] stage of development as those of electricity in the early days of Marconi and Edison"; yet even the rude beginnings of nonviolent resistance met with success. That seems to be the crucial lesson in their forgotten history.

A notable comparison might throw that lesson into relief: The population of India was a little under 400 million during the period when Gandhi and his co-workers roused the country to a sustained non-violent resistance. In this struggle, a few hundred of these 400 million and a handful of British nationals lost their lives; many thousands of

Indians spent years in prison, which Gandhi had predicted would be the price of the country's freedom. At the end India emerged not only independent but, considering the shock of the partition with Pakistan and the condition of her economy, also reasonably stable. Its mode of resistance had trained the nation for self-government rather than for war. Today India has overcome the drain of two centuries of exploitation and is exporting both food and skills as well as some manufactures. Her young democracy, which tolerates communist opposition on one side and right-wing elements on the other, has weathered serious political crises. India has become a voice for the nonaligned nations and has begun to piece together the historical destiny of which Gandhi dreamed.

Shortly after India's independence a smaller colonial nation gained its freedom but by very different methods. Algeria, in 1962, had a population of 11 million. Of these 11 million, 800,000, nearly one in thirteen, died in the violent struggle against French rule. Hundreds of thousands here also spent years in prisons and concentration camps, and the beleaguered French regime at times resorted to inhuman methods. The Algerian economy has still not recovered, nor has the country found political stability. Democracy there is marginal. Control passed to a militaristic "strong man," and guerrilla fighting has continued among various factions, complicating the territorial squabbles with Morocco. This dismal outcome was not the result of any difference in the mentalities of the imperial powers but of the great difference in the respective resisters' methods.

History also teaches the shrewd observer why nonviolence works. A common pattern of resistance movements since World War II has been that the occupation troops refuse to fire on nonviolent demonstrators as long as the latter remain nonviolent. Fresh troops have to be rushed to the scene and ordered to start firing before they can strike up a relationship with the insurgents, which usually frightens the latter out of their nonviolent posture and into the attacker's mode of operation, where they are quickly overcome. Dramatic instances of this have occurred in Hungary, Czechoslovakia, and in East Germany in 1953, about which the authors of *Speak Truth to Power* point out:

> We [the United States] were so preoccupied with power concepts that one of the most striking aspects of the uprisings was largely overlooked: *the fact that a group of Russian soldiers refused to fire on the unarmed and*

nonviolent demonstrators. Not only were the demonstrators spared violence, but a number of their grievances were recognized and corrected. How can this outcome be squared with the familiar argument that only naked power is respected by the Russians?

When we are not "preoccupied with power concepts" we can see that some sense of kinship with their fellow beings persists somehow in all people, no matter how indoctrinated. Nonviolence, especially when it is persistent, appeals to that sense, which is always present in everyone, and therefore succeeds where other methods fail or "work" in only limited ways and often at the cost of grievous suffering.

To be thus preoccupied, on the other hand, is to misread human nature. Not only will we overlook or misconstrue much that has happened in history, not only will we miss the significance of our adversaries' behavior—as we did in the case just cited—but we will completely fail to understand the nature of our present crisis.

WHERE DO WE STAND NOW?

A long history stands behind those Soviet troops who "failed" to fire on the unarmed demonstrators in East Berlin. In centuries gone by, rum had to be issued to soldiers to "enable" them to fight. It has always been difficult to get "otherwise 'trained' troops," says the *Report from Iron Mountain*, "to fire at an enemy close enough to be recognized as an individual rather than simply a target"—our old issue of alienation. But in Korea, and even more so in Vietnam, this "difficulty" reached critical proportions. If modern war were not fought at such impersonal distances, or if the Vietnamese had not fought back so hard, giving us a convincing reason to fight them, it is doubtful we could have waged a land war against them very long. Those who did wage it for us came home with appalling psychological disabilities. Why is the modern soldier so dispirited?

To look at the modern attitude to war is to look at a picture of immense confusion. On the one hand, there has never been such a profusion of peace activities. Some have long traditions, like the Fellowship of Reconciliation (going back to the Quakers) or the Women's International League for Peace and Freedom. Many others are brand-new: the American Committee on East-West Accord, a galaxy of distinguished professionals dedicated to détente between the United

States and the U.S.S.R.; Amnesty International, which has made headlines as an international group striving to preserve human rights; the People's Peace Movement in Ireland; the World Constitution and Parliament Association; the Center for War/Peace Studies; Global Education Associates; Pax World Fund, with assets of $5 million, which invests its shareholders' money in "firms producing life-supportive products and services"; the World Peace Tax Fund, which is seeking legislation that would allow conscientious objectors to pay the military portion of their income taxes to an alternative peace-building organization; Peace Brigades International, which is promoting an unarmed volunteer UN peace-making service; and literally hundreds more. In 1978, almost 200 years after President Washington first suggested it, President Carter set up a commission to study the possibility of a national academy for peace, and now President Reagan is studying their proposal.

On the other hand, we all know that militarism and the threat of international war is also increasing. President Carter also submitted the largest military budget in human history and reinstated registration for the draft. About 200,000 scientists in this country are working on military research and development, while perhaps 200 are paid to work on peace-related projects of any kind. In education, Congress recently increased from 1,200 to 1,600 the number of JROTC units, whose avowed purpose it is to instill military values and perspectives in high school students (shades of M. Lavisse!); massive public outcry was needed recently to block the establishment of what would have been the nation's first public high school–level military academy in Cincinnati.

The reason for this confusion has been most clearly put by Professor Boulding: War has been delegitimated, but peace has not yet been legitimated. The same could be said of every other form of violence. Therefore, to know how peace and nonviolence can be legitimated is the most important question facing every human being of our age. The cases we have looked at in this chapter suggest that the answer lies in learning how to awaken the latent and neglected sense of kinship in the individual and how to spread that sense throughout society and its institutions.

I have not tried to give a balanced view of history here, rather a balancing view; that is, I have tried to counterbalance the distorted outlook that prevails "not because historians are perverse," as educator

Patricia Mische has explained, but because war, the preparations for war, and the outcome of war "usually result in swift and identifiable change"—and because we are preoccupied with physical power, predisposed to a fatalistic interpretation of our options. The only balanced view, as Norman Cousins often says, is that "nobody knows enough to be a pessimist." There is nothing in human history—not our evolution, not our aboriginal prehistory, not our recent past—that says we cannot eliminate violence. There is much, indeed, to indicate that we can and must do so, and in our time. The question is how.

6 | The Home-Team Strategy

*This way you have chosen to escape your troubles will not
work, nor would it be a worthy one; there is only one way
which is practical and good—not to be hindering
others but to improve yourselves.*

Socrates

*To renounce winning brings to oneself the goods that
cannot be lost.*

Jorge Waxemberg

At a pro football game during the 1976 season a rather common
mishap took an unusual turn. A Cleveland player had purposely
slammed into an opposing quarterback, throwing him to the ground
with serious injuries to the neck and back. But as the injured man was
being carried off to the ambulance, the player who had hit him, rather
shaken by what he had done, ran up alongside the gurney and said, "I'm
sorry, man. I just got caught up in the game." Can this give us a clue to
how we get involved in violence and how to cure it?

CAUGHT IN THE GAME

Many behavioral scientists have studied games and sports for clues
to what causes violence and war. There can certainly be a ready connection between them. It was not unknown for British soldiers to
kick a soccer ball ahead of them as they began attacks on German
positions in World War I. Captain W. P. Nevill, for example, launched
his company's advance that way in the fruitless attack on the Somme in
July, 1916. (Captain Nevill was instantly killed.) In 1969 a soccer match
between El Salvador and Honduras led to a real shooting war in which
1,000 people were killed.

Modern sports are themselves plagued with violence, and the plague
is contagious. When fights break out between two hockey players, for
example, they can spread to the entire opposing teams, then "empty the

benches" of even the inactive players, and finally empty the stands. The violent potential of sports is eagerly exploited by promoters in the profession and in the media, a dangerously inflammatory practice. Not only does it make the sports themselves more violent, but, as one sportscaster put it, "How [do] you limit the violence to the playing field?"

One reason violence spreads from the playing field to the stands (and from the stands to the playing field) so easily is close at hand: We are making the same mistakes about violence in both realms. Both in the game of sports and the game of life we try to use a certain amount or a certain kind of violence and hope that it does not spread, that the genie will come out of the bottle and do only what we consciously ask of it. "Right or wrong, violence is an integral part of sports," says one sportswriter; a retired player owns that he likes football because of its "terrific combination of violence and science" (which, by the way, would be a good description of modern war). There is nothing wrong with this attitude, another commentator explains. Football contains a necessary element of "good" violence, consisting of the "most violent, aggressive action a player could take in the course of carrying out his *responsibility* on a play" (my emphasis). But we all deplore it when this "good" violence spills over into what he calls the unnecessary, or "gratuitous," type—the type associated with Dan White when he unaccountably used violence against the community that taught it to him. But all violence is senseless and gratuitous, as we have seen. The error here is the same as relying on the death penalty to limit homicide (and having no conceptual framework with which to understand that it has no such effect).

What would make for sports and games that have *no* violence?—for there are such sports and games, as I have already mentioned. It is a question of values. Terry Orlick, author of *Winning Through Cooperation*, remarked about the absence of bitterness and intragroup rivalry and the complete absence of violence among Chinese sports men and women to the chairman of the All-China Sports Federation, who told him, "Winning and losing is only temporary, friendship is eternal." Among the !Kung, at least until recently, ritual games and dances were enjoyed by all the people, coming and going as they liked, always trying to improve themselves but never striving to compete against anyone else in the community. There is no such thing as a game without an element of competition. But sports and games that do not produce violence have an *entirely different axis of competition* than those that do: not competition against others, not a desire to "win" where somebody else has got to lose, but simply a desire to do better, a competition against the drawbacks in oneself.

There is evidence that nature intended this kind of play to have a role in the evolution of all social animals. All such species, including *Homo sapiens*, need symbols to communicate their intentions to one another and are themselves locked into a symbolic network that shapes their perception of reality. Nature works with this communicative capacity to produce cooperation. In a well-known series of experiments, psychologists Margaret and Harry Harlow raised a group of monkeys normally in every respect except that they were not allowed to play with age-mates. These monkeys grew up dangerously deficient in social competence. They picked on animals much more powerful than themselves; and had they been out in the wild where they needed to cooperate for food and for protection, they would probably not have survived. Similarly for human beings, to quote Marie Winn:

> Losing gracefully, learning to give in, getting along peacefully with others, all these are skills that children develop as they learn to play successfully with other children. The survival value of such skills in human adult life is obvious, although international wars and intrasocial violence attest to . . . imperfect attainment of them.

The way we play games in most modern societies and how these games shape our attitudes and relationships stand in violent contrast to nature's benign purpose. Coaches work themselves into red-faced rages, biting their towels and weeping tears of frustration if their teams are not "winning." Twelve-year-olds are taught to cheat and to despise their teammates at any sign of "weakness." Worst of all, they are regularly "psyched up" before each game to hate their opponents, without regard for what this does permanently to their own psyches. This is called "winning is everything," and to read the description of it in William Bruns's and Thomas Tutko's well-documented exposé is to agree with the authors that we have erected on that ethic, "with parental sanction, a program of child abuse." Players themselves say, "The tyranny of competition takes all the fun out of it."

Sports as we play them, emphasizing the aggressive element and gradually fixing on that reason for playing to the exclusion of all other reasons, reflect and strengthen the competitive tendency inherent in our (as in any) culture. This is the same effect produced by the violence in the media, gratuitously heightening our aggression against one another at the expense of everything else that a relationship can mean. We have deified this value and enshrined it in all our cultural institutions. Even in marriage, the deepest symbol and most important form of unity in all human cultures, the idea that one must "get something out of" the relationship, legal contracts made between husband and wife, and the fatal idea of competition have taken hold. In describing politics we now use sport (or military) metaphors extensively, because the political process has been nearly reduced to a brute selection of "winners," a kind of social Darwinian survival of the most aggressive. The eve of the 1980 presidential election produced a political cartoon showing the contenders, Carter and Reagan, as gunslingers facing each other down on the deserted street of a Western town, about to draw. One total winner; one dead loser. But this clever cartoon failed to show the real losers—the people, the American political process. How can you build community by polarizing and dividing?

There is an even more ominous side to this obsession. The irrational mentality behind our foreign policy, too, as John K. Galbraith has described it, "never asks why we are competing with the Chinese or the Soviets in Vietnam or elsewhere. Or what we accomplish. The competition itself is the only and sufficient thing." President Johnson himself summarized the purpose behind our country's involvement in Southeast Asia in the ringing phrase: "We are the number one nation, and we are going to stay the number one nation." He might have been echoing the chant that could be heard (and still can, of course) from the winning side in any Midwestern football stadium, "We're number one, we're number one." Or he might have been echoing—though he was less likely to know this—a remark attributed to the German Kaiser: "We do not desire war, we only desire victory." From the human tragedy of exploitative marriage to the global catastrophe of politics, all our institutions have come to reflect an attitude of divisive squabble. We have indeed begun to manifest what social psychologist Elliot Aronson called "a staggering cultural obsession with victory."

Which is to say, we are all "caught up in the game." Where there is obsession, there cannot be judgment. Competition is the first step in the symbolic "game." Whenever competition comes into the relationship between two parties, they start losing sight of their own best interests. "When the problem has a tinge of competitiveness," says Professor Howard Raiffa of Harvard, "analysis is shunned."

The road to violence begins in competition against others. Competition leads to rivalry, which magnifies the "otherness" of others until that delusion is so intense that conflict and violence are the natural result. Shortly after the outbreak of World War I, few people could remember what the great struggle was about, but that did not prevent 10 million combatants and many thousands of noncombatants from perishing before everyone could agree that one of the sides had "won."

But anyone who wants to avoid competition immediately faces two serious questions. Competition and conflict are all around us. What do we do about it? If we do not make up our minds to win, what *are* we going to do? Lose? If we try to extend our circle of compassion farther outward to include those who consider themselves enemies, won't they take advantage of our apparent weakness? And second, we evolved by struggle; we have a billion-year evolutionary momentum of aggression behind us. Do we just clench our fists and try to block it? What becomes of our anger? Let's take up these important questions in turn.

NOT ME AGAINST YOU . . .

We have found that when we start seeing relationships through the "game" of competition—a semipermanent condition in the West— one of the first unpleasant consequences is that "analysis is shunned": Options are closed down, and everything begins to appear as what it is not. It follows that a first step out of this game is to keep reminding ourselves that there is—always, in every conflict—a major option we are tending to forget, an option that is neither fight nor flight, the option of *resolution.*

In the realm of conflict resolution we meet some modest examples of what our civilization is doing *right* about violence. There is nothing new about conflict resolution; in a sense nature, as we have seen, has been practicing it for eons. Turnbull observed that among the Mbuti intracommunal disputes became the concern of anyone in the village and were settled "with little reference to the alleged rights and wrongs of the case, but chiefly with the intention of restoring peace to the community." During the thirteenth century it became a high diplomatic art to keep hotheaded lords from attacking one another, an art usually practiced by intermediaries who were kin of both sides or represented church authority.

Not surprisingly, the violence of our own conflict-ridden age has stimulated the search for new ways to use this noble science. The International Peace Academy, an independent agency that grew indirectly out of UN peace-keeping experiences, trains top-level military and diplomatic personnel from all over the world (114 countries per year, as of 1979) in the arts of peace-seeking negotiation. The training, in today's symbolic style, includes a good deal of role playing and imagining oneself in the other fellow's shoes. On the other end of the scale, a follower of Gandhi, Vinobha Bhave, has called for a nongovernmental, peace-keeping "army" of 600,000 unarmed volunteers, and a grass-roots international organization has been formed to meet this challenge.

We can also take an example that is not from international conflict at all and with it illustrate some principles of how these efforts work. Under the U.S. Civil Rights Act of 1964, the federal Community Relations Service was set up to offer mediation "whenever, in its judgment, peaceful relations among citizens of a community are threatened by racial/ethnic conflict." Some 1,200 cases a year fall into this category. In about one-fifth of these the CRS can ultimately bring both sides to a mutually satisfactory formal agreement, while in most of the others they are helpful but in a less conclusive way. News clips about the CRS leave little doubt what the presence of federal mediators contributes. They facilitate *communication*: "Sometimes it's enough just to get the two sides talking and they resolve their differences." (Santa Rosa, California) There is *trust*: "Once people sit across the table and get to know each other, they develop an element of trust. Once this happens, they can find a way to live and work together." (Chicago, Illinois) There is *respect* and *understanding*: "The Monroe reformatory agreement includes a provision to add cultural awareness training to orientation for new staff." (San Antonio, Texas) These qualities are the stuff of conflict resolution.

Yet all of these efforts remain, as I have indicated, only modestly successful. The 20 percent success rate of the CRS, for example, while it saves taxpayers millions of dollars in futile and community-destroying forms of violence, cannot by itself, as the regional director confided in me, outweigh the forces that are causing violence to increase.

Two of the limitations of this method are obvious. Arbitration, or mediation, or reconciliation—the three professionally recognized forms of the technique—all require the intervention of a third party. How often is a skilled third-party mediator available? How often is one invited? Mediation efforts are only feasible when both parties in the conflict are willing to have a mediator, which means that whole classes of conflict are beyond the reach of this technique. Ask any police officer why he or she does not like to respond to a call from neighbors when a fight has broken out between husband and wife. These are statistically among the most dangerous police calls, because the couple often turn their fury on the intruder—and the fury released when an intense emotional relationship is coming apart is no joke. Second, mediation of whatever kind can only come into play *after* violent elements in an interaction are already operating; that is, it can head off violence, sometimes, but it cannot *prevent* violence at the earlier stages of competition, enmity, or conflict (except in the indirect way that any kind of caring improves the general atmosphere). It is too far "downstream."

There is, however, a way to employ the principle of these good offices of the mediator without suffering its limitations. Here again, a simple illustration may be helpful.

The greatest soccer player of the century, and one of the greatest sportsmen of all time, is Pelé, superstar of the Brazilian Santos. Pelé is an unusual human being. The whole "game" of fame and money never seems to have affected his childlike simplicity. He has always refused to do ads for alcohol or cigarettes, for example, saying, "I love kids." And on his last exhibition match between his new team, the New York Cosmos, and his team of many years, the Santos, he made a beautiful symbolic statement: He played his heart out for the Cosmos up until half time, then went over to the Santos and played just as hard for them. For Pelé there was no "versus" in the competition; he was competing only with himself. Almost like the !Kung, for Pelé there was no question of home team against visitors, because both teams were home teams for him. No one was offended by the gesture; everybody "won."

And now to look at the deadliest game of all. You probably remember that during Thanksgiving week, November, 1977, the late President Sadat of Egypt made a surprise visit of state to Jerusalem, breaching the apparently impenetrable deadlock of tension between two nations who had called each other natural enemies since the days of the Bible and warred against each another four times in the space of thirty years. Many people no more understood the significance of the event than they were able to predict it. But an astute observer, James Reston, in an article aptly titled, "Beyond Self-Defense in the Middle East," understood it perfectly:

> When Sadat and Begin sought to define the things that unite their peoples rather than the things that divide them, each in his own way turned from the secular world to the nobler religious ideals of the holy city where they met. . . . And the disbelieving world now asks who won—as if this were a football game.

Sadat, like Pelé, was an unusual person. His widow, Jehan Sadat, feels that "women are the natural enemies of war," and she has made important contributions to peace in connection with the Irish Women for Peace movement (now the People's Peace Movement) and elsewhere. Sadat too saw, as his act of heroism shows, that the welfare of Egypt had to be sought in the welfare of the whole world. If he did not live to see the fruits of this vision, nonetheless he helped bring it closer to those who, as Reston says, still cannot see past the narrow, polarizing framework of the conflict game.

The way to use mediation with potentially unlimited effectiveness, then, so that it can lead to a condition of zero violence? *Be your own mediator.* Personal style is the beginning, a style in which the mediator's detachment is, so to speak, internalized. And the way to get upstream with this technique is by striving to use it constantly, not waiting until conflict and violence have erupted. A life style informed by this technique means facing others with an entirely different attitude than that encouraged by modern conditions and modern conditioning, an especially difficult task when we feel the configuration of conflict closing in. The "enemy" flag evokes the "win" response; a mind-set dedicated to "winning" sees—and produces—abundant enemies. We have to change that mind-set to one of learning and coevolving in the teeth of our own conditioned responses to experience true "winning through cooperation." This gives an idea of the magnitude of the change we have to bring about in ourselves—and also of the magnitude of the effective power released when we do so. To listen unfailingly to an "opponent's" point of view—indeed even to recognize that he or she *has* a point of view—is a powerful mechanism for resolution.

As the examples of Pelé, Sadat, and others show clearly, we can keep all these attitude changes in mind with a simple formula.

NOT ME AGAINST YOU, BUT ME AND YOU AGAINST THE PROBLEM

In marriage, obviously, "husband against wife" is a destructive delusion. No less so management against labor, white against black, or nation against nation. Clearly we are all in this together. Husband and wife are both on the home team, estrangement is the visitor; white and black are both the community, racism is the destructive intruder; and of course all nations must learn to inhabit the earth together in the face of their common enemy, war. This could be called a home-team strategy, a realistic attitude that arises from trusting our own inkling that all life is one and results not in victory for one side and loss for any other but in progress for all.

Yes, we are always and everywhere in conflict today; but that means we are everywhere presented with opportunities. Every conflict is an opportunity for a higher resolution. Once we have succeeded in adopting a home-team strategy, we do not have to dread conflict any more. We do not seek conflict out; but if it comes, by refusing to be caught up in the game of winning we can use the home-team strategy as leverage toward reconciliation.

Yes, there are always differences among human individuals and human groups. But differences do not have to divide people. Resources, territory, and ideologies are not the sources but merely the occasions of conflict; the sources are in the human propensity to see one side of an issue as "mine." Without that propensity no issue need become a conflict; with it, even a symbolic issue like a college football game can erupt into a riot.

Georgi A. Arbatov, Director of the Moscow Institute for American and Canadian Studies, made this statement at the 30th Pugwash Conference of 1978:

> I believe that there is increasing need to understand that the Soviet Union and the United States, East and West, face ... an impersonal adversary that overrides any specific threat one side may see in the other.

This adversary is the looming danger of nuclear war. With all our differences and contradictions we have an overwhelming mutual interest in seeking to avert the threat of war.

What is our alternative if we do *not* take this new way of seeing? Victory? Can there be victory in a nuclear holocaust? No, we will simply earn the fate of a species that cannot learn the lesson of history, the lesson that was described so well by the writer Edmund Blunden as he contemplated the disaster of the Somme, on July 1, 1916, when sixty thousand British soldiers fell in the inconclusive assault: "No road. No thoroughfare. Neither race had won, nor could win, the War. The War had won, and would go on winning."

THE CONVERSION OF EVOLUTIONARY POTENTIAL

What happens psychologically to individuals who do not express their inherited tendencies to anger and aggression?

One winter evening near the beginning of our century a dignified young Indian boarded the overnight train from Durban, South Africa, to Pretoria, and took his seat in a first-class compartment. At the mountain station of Maritzburg a European passenger entered the compartment, gave his brown fellow traveler a dour look, and withdrew. Moments later he was back with two railway officials who told the young lawyer he would have to leave. "But I have a first-class ticket," Gandhi protested. No matter. He would have to leave. But he refused to go, saying that if they wanted him out of the compartment they would have to drag him out by force. The officials pulled Gandhi from the compartment and set him out on the platform, doubtless expecting that he would climb back into a third-class coach. But this man who many years later, as a mahatma ("great soul," or savior), would refuse to travel in first-class accommodations, did not move. Throughout the night he sat where he was on the station platform, not even asking for his overcoat (which officials were holding with the rest of his baggage), afraid of provoking a further humiliation, shivering with cold and indignation in the mountain air.

In later years Gandhi was wont to call this episode the most creative of his life. Why? Because of the titanic emotional struggle he waged within himself. Should he go back to India and leave this land of insults? Or should he get his firm to hale the railway company into court? Either way, how would it solve the problem? No, this was not a personal insult to himself, to M. K. Gandhi; it was even more than an offense to the Indian community of South Africa. This was human cruelty in all its nakedness—and he vowed to fight it.

This decision changed modern history. It was much more than a change of mind, because underneath that change of attitude, the decision not to react personally or yield to the peevish demands for private satisfaction, underneath the decision to direct his anger at the *problem*, not at the people caught in it, was the beginning of an immense psychic transformation. Decades later, Gandhi was to describe this transformation scientifically: "I have learnt through bitter experience the one supreme lesson to conserve my anger, and as heat conserved is transmuted into energy, even so our anger controlled can be transmuted into a power which can move the world."

Everyone who had the privilege of knowing Gandhi in later life remarked on his immense energy, love, and joy. Back in India, he worked fifteen hours a day, seven days a week, for more than thirty years. On shipboard on his way to London for the Round Table Conference in 1931 he wrote until his hand was cramped, then switched to his left hand and wrote more. In London he averaged four hours' sleep a night, often getting by with less, sometimes with none. He kept five secretaries and a special typist on the go. The burly Scotland Yard men assigned to his protection complained that they couldn't keep up with him on his walks. Through all this his daily cotton spinning and prayer meetings were never interrupted, even during Parliamentary sessions. "We keep telling him to slow down," said one of his anxious doctors, "but he pays no attention."

And yet in all this activity, he showed no trace of being *driven*. When effort was not necessary, as at times on shipboard going to or from the conference, he slept like a baby. Apparently the titanic pace agreed with him. When asked her dominant impression of the man alongside whom she had worked for many years, Ashadevi Aryanayakam uttered three words, "His great love." Everyone knew this about Gandhi; you could see it in his eyes. "I was almost taken aback by the gaiety in them," writes William Shirer. "This was a man inwardly secure, who, despite the burden he carried, the hardships he had endured, could chuckle at man's foibles, including his own."

Gandhi himself attributed all these psychological benefits—the energy, the love, the joy—directly to the struggle to control his anger that had begun that winter's evening on the railway platform at Maritzburg and continued throughout his life: "Such a struggle leaves one stronger for it. The more I work at this law [of nonviolence], the more I feel the delight in my life, the delight in the scheme of the universe. It gives me a peace and a meaning of the mysteries of nature that I have no power to describe."

We have seen that when confronted with hostility, we have a choice of behavior that lies between fight and flight—namely, nonviolent resolution, which resolves the external difference and reintegrates the ruptured relationship. Correspondingly, to deal with our own anger we have a choice that is *neither* expression nor repression. We have the choice of *converting* anger to positive action, in a word, to love. And just as the in-between and often overlooked choice of resolution integrates relationships, the difficult choice of love heals the alienated personality from within. The change involved is difficult, often very deep. It seems to be more a restoration of or a reconversion to our original condition than a plain conversion, which perhaps explains why its impact on us is so healthy. As Gandhi declared, "My noncooperation *has its roots* not in hatred but in love."

It is worth being very clear about this transformation, because it is so different from either choice we tend to recognize under the tense conditions of modern living. The latest book from the innate aggression school is being advertised with the provocative question, "Can we deny our million-year-old inheritance" of anger and aggression? No one is asking us to deny it. Imagine, to continue Gandhi's scientific model, that you are a powerful steam engine at a railway station, in whom the healthy fire is building up a great head of pressure. What are your choices? You can pretend it isn't there, repression, with which you run the grave danger of exploding or doing slower forms of damage to your system. You can open all the safety valves, expression, which merely scalds everyone standing around you. Or you can let all that steam drive your evolutionary gears and start you rolling forward. Once you've learned to get the rust out of your system, you could be flying along in delirious freedom as Gandhi was, doing yourself and the world a tremendous lot of good.

One of the horrors of the modern age has been the attempt to contain violence by forcibly suppressing anger through "scientific" techniques such as the Pavlovian conditioning of human beings (popularized in the novel and then the film, *Clockwork Orange*), the use of anger-suppressing drugs, and, finally, psychosurgery. What most offends here is not so much the gross superstition involved—as if a person's anger can be lopped out with a portion of his or her anatomy—or even the attempt to subvert that individual's own responsibility. What offends most is that to the extent that such invasive techniques can derail the capacity for anger, to that extent, they block the capacity for love. For at base these capacities are the same, as Gandhi's reconversion illustrates.

A medical friend of mine who worked at Stanford in the early 1970s noticed that the wards of the student health center (the same wards that had taken in victims of psychedelic bad-tripping in the previous decade) were filled with victims of T-groups and eyeball-to-eyeball encounter sessions. It is interesting that the same era that produced the extreme of suppression in one sector of society, the advocates of psychosurgery and the like, produced the extreme of expression in another, with the harmful results that my friend observed. Both expression and suppression are based on inadequate psychological theories. Even if Gandhi were the only one—and we have already seen that he was not—his sole example is enough to show that there is another, safer way to deal with anger: what I have called a home-team strategy, based on human beings' innate capacity to transform anger into love.

This strategy is far from a utopian suggestion. It does not presuppose a world free from competition but a progressive change to a world in which the competitive impulse is not at the service of divisive egoism. Thus, in the political arena, ideas compete; in the marketplace, products compete. This is healthy. Only *people* will not compete, meaning they will not compete *against one another*; rather, like the !Kung players, they will compete against themselves. They will compete with their own aggressive egoism, with whatever robs them of the fierce joys of unity and cooperation. In this sense life will indeed be a struggle to excel, but not a struggle to dominate others.

This struggle will assuredly hold out a kind of victory, not victory over others but at last the definitive victory over violence, starting right where it begins. Anger is an extremely destructive force, and the disposition toward anger is a liability no human being can escape. But what is the real psychological nature of that disposition? Freud showed that anger wells up from the unconscious, where it is a primal constituent of our biological make-up. Yes, Gandhi would say, but dig deeper. Underneath anger, there is love. Which will predominate in our minds and actions is a matter of human choice.

Part Three

THE
HIGHEST
GOAL

7 | The Acid Test: War and Peace

Thus always we are daunted by the appearances; not seeing that their whole value lies at bottom in the state of mind. It is really a thought that built this portentous war establishment, and a thought shall also melt it away. Observe the ideas of the present day—orthodoxy, skepticism, missions, popular education, temperance, anti-masonry, antislavery; see how each of these abstractions has embodied itself in an imposing apparatus in the community; and how timber, brick, lime and stone have flown into convenient shape, obedient to the master idea reigning in the minds of many persons.

Emerson

The belief that we can achieve security through armaments . . . is . . . a disastrous illusion.

Einstein

Unless we can apply all the strategies we have been discussing to the worst case of violence—war—all we have said thus far will be whistling in the wind. Why worry about a crime rate, or a divorce rate, or cancer, or alienation when everything we are trying to preserve from crime and alienation may be blasted out of existence in thirty minutes? I have been saying that the key to the elimination of all forms of violence lies in the individual. But in war, the individual's destructiveness is multiplied a million times over, and the individual's capacity to prevent war would seem to be almost nothing. How can we hope to eliminate international war with the strategies I have been suggesting? Let me back into this question by taking a look at the methods we are using now.

Our present strategy for keeping a nuclear holocaust at bay is called deterrence. It rests entirely on the idea that we have—and can project the fact that we have—a "second strike capability": If the enemy launched nuclear missiles at us we could still inflict damage that they would consider unacceptable on them. Leaving aside other strategies of which one hears occasional rumors (that Defense Department planners are actually building up a pre-emptive first strike capability), this is the basic "posture" we are presently using to guard our national security.

As an example of how the deterrence strategy works people often point to the Cuban missile crisis. This was the "finest hour" of the cold war: The Soviets were putting missiles 90 miles from our shores, and with a determined show of military capability the president forced them to back down. It's easy to breathe a sigh of relief about how our military muscle is keeping war from our doorstep when we think about this incident—but only if we think about it in that one way. If we remember that in this as in every conflict there must be another side to the story, if we remember that actions can have unpredictable consequences reaching far beyond the immediate ones we anticipate, the picture is not so rosy. The following quotations, the first from unidentified sources within the Soviet Union and the second from a Soviet deputy foreign minister, give a sobering impression of how *they* perceived and reacted to the Cuban missile crisis:

> At the end of World War II Truman ordered the Soviets out of Persia in 48 hours and we went. After all, you had the atom bomb. In the 1950's you were stronger than us militarily. In 1962 you made us back down on Cuba. But we told ourselves it would never happen again.

> The Soviet Union was forced to uncover and display the outgoing missiles for visual proof of their withdrawal and counting. American reconnaissance planes swooped down in insultingly close range, just over the masts of the Soviet freighters headed homeward on a humbling journey. . . .
> You Americans will never be able to do this to us again.

Our continuous threatening of the Soviets for thirty-five years (or more than sixty, if you count the landing of U.S. Marines in Siberia in 1919) has had the effect of continuously goading them and hardening their determination to "beat" us. Our show of force over Cuba did cause them to withdraw the missiles, but what else did it do? In the long run, it added to our insecurity. In evaluating our "success" in the Cuba crisis, we forgot that the Russians are people too, just like us; that they react badly to being bullied, just as we would. We forgot their side of the conflict—and we still forget. Not long ago General George S. Brown, Chairman of the Joint Chiefs of Staff, declared that the "sheer massiveness of Soviet strategic nuclear programs is staggering." What about the massiveness of *our* strategic nuclear programs? Doesn't it stagger the Russians? Aren't they going to react by making their programs even more staggering?

Professor Herbert York, former head of Lawrence Livermore Radiation Laboratories and U.S. arms control negotiator, has pointed out that virtually every Soviet weapon that threatens our security today, "and indeed our existence," was invented or perfected right here in this country—to threaten the existence of the Soviets.

This is the bilateral myopia of the cold war (or of any aggravated conflict). We feel reassured by our capacity for violence but frightened of the enemy's; we forget that the feeling must be mutual. We forget, for example, that in 1962 we had already placed ballistic missiles much closer than ninety miles from Soviet borders. We forget that every time we "succeed" in a show of force, our own military reflexes are reinforced, which impedes our freedom to choose and reason. But most of all, we forget that deterrence contains the seeds of its own destruction. As we have already seen, in discussing the death penalty, you can only deter someone with a threat of retaliation if that person stops to calculate the costs and benefits of attacking you. "A mad or irrational adversary," writes Indian scholar G. D. Deshingkar, "cannot be deterred." And if your way of deterring the others is to threaten them, *you are making them less rational* each time you do so, and thus making the mechanics of deterrence less effective. Such a policy cannot succeed for long. To frighten your adversary is to put yourself in danger, and frightening our adversaries is the sum and substance of our present policy for avoiding war.

But deterrence is even more two-edged than this. To frighten those whom we have made our enemies, policy makers need us to be afraid *of* them. We have to be "psyched up" like twelve-year-olds before a basketball game; hence, General Brown's remark about the "staggering" Soviet build-up and so many remarks like it. Senate minority leader Arthur Vandenberg set the program at the initiation of the cold war: We will have to "scare the hell out of the country."

Many studies show that animals are well equipped to deal with an occasional crisis. Adrenalin can galvanize the physical organism—for a while. But if the crisis drags on too long, it can make the organism very sick. Rats swim like champions when their adrenalin output has been speeded up by cutting off their whiskers, but if they have to swim for a long period, they give out much sooner than rats whose systems have not been challenged in that way. So it is with the hypertensive American business executive and other go-getters who succumb to the strains of competition in their early forties. Clearly there are parallels to be found in the state of deadly competition that has gripped the rival superpowers who felt that they emerged victorious from the ashes of World War II: By trying to live in a constant state of tension these nations are making themselves economically, politically, and socially sick.

Between 1946, when Senator Vandenberg made that remark about the fear crusade, and 1975, the United States spent $1.6 *trillion* on what we choose to call defense, only to spend as much again from 1975 to 1981. This expenditure has exerted a steady upward pressure on domestic prices, more serious in the long run than that caused by the insubordination of oil-producing nations. It has caused unemployment: According to Senator Kennedy, speaking in 1977, the annual military expenditure of $107 billion took away the economic base for over a million jobs that could have been sustained in more stable and less capital-intensive occupations. Professor Kenneth Boulding has estimated that at least 50 percent of our economic difficulty is caused by what he calls this unusable military "cancer," without reference to the political impact of our prolonged crisis of "security" or the psychological state of young people who feel there isn't going to be a future.

One of the clearest symptoms of the sickness brought on by a state of protracted crisis is the story of "civil defense." Civil defense is neither civil nor does it defend. No sooner did American homeowners start to build bomb shelters than those "shelters" turned into weapons turned against ourselves. Civil defense coordinators and military men began publicly warning people to stock their shelters with loaded shotguns as the best way to repel—not foreigners, but their own less foresighted (or less patriotic) neighbors. Southern Californians hired Spanish-speaking workers so their neighbors would not know they were building shelters; while across the border in Nevada, Kern County officials prepared measures that were uncivil indeed, to repel any Angelinos who might try to flee from the bombs in their direction. Fallout shelters and air-raid drills became the focus for a generation of protestors who could not stomach crawling into holes in the ground to protect themselves. They pointed out that this so-called defensive system would tend to provoke war by signaling our willingness to engage in conflict, not an implausible interpretation, since that was just how we were being told to regard the similar but cruder efforts at civil defense in Moscow. In any city struck by a modern hydrogen bomb all the central inhabitants would probably be asphyxiated by the fire storm. In the country, it is doubtful that people could live long enough in a shelter to escape the radioactive fallout or that there would still be a life-supporting world to crawl back out to.

No less fanatical was the idea that we could be protected by antiballistic missiles, which would shoot down Soviet missiles for us, the way Wonder Woman deflects bullets with her magic bracelets. Eight billion dollars were spent on this vain imagining, yet as political scientist Lloyd Dumas has said, "There is no such thing as an effective defense of any kind against a nuclear attack." Admiral Gene LaRocque, formerly a Pentagon planner and now head of the Center for Defense Information, confirms this: "Thirty minutes' flight time from the Soviet Union—or fifteen minutes from the submarines sitting off the coast right now with nuclear weapons aimed at Boston and New York. And there is no defense against Soviet missiles, absolutely none."

THE WINDS OF UTAH

We are living in a climate that, as Richard J. Barnet of the Institute for Policy Studies has put it, "chokes rational thought." Psychologists have shown that in a crisis, as at Three Mile Island, the participants cannot make decisions with anything like the necessary courage or imagination—and we have been in a crisis far too long. That is why we think we have "no choice" but to escalate, no choice but to stay ahead, why we never think about how our escalations affect the other side, why we swallow so much gobbledegook and try not to notice that it's crazy: "One of the basic techniques of arms control, paradoxically, is to improve the military forces"; "we had to destroy the village in order to save it"; "if you want peace, prepare for war." That is also why, while we agree with those who say that we need "peace through strength," it never dawns on us that there is a strength other than readiness to kill. We have also closed our eyes to a terrible thing that is happening to this country.

In 1954 John Wayne made one of his characteristic movies, *The Conqueror*, with Agnes Moorehead, Susan Hayward, and Lee Van Cleef, on a set in Utah. Director Dick Powell was a perfectionist; he wanted that red dirt of the Utah desert and had several tons of it trucked back to the studio, where the cast members traipsed around in it for two years to finish the $6 million film. No one told them that about a year earlier, just after 5:05 A.M. on May 19, 1953, when an atomic bomb had been tested over nearby Nevada, the winds had unpredictably shifted and blown a huge cloud of radioactive fallout into Utah, depositing it on the town of St. George and the nearby desert that was soon to be the scene of *The Conqueror*.

John Wayne died of his second cancer in June, 1979. Dick Powell died of cancer in 1963. Agnes Moorehead (1974), Susan Hayward (1975), co-star Pedro Armangariz (committed suicide while in the hospital for cancer treatment, 1963), production manager Harold Lewis and his wife, Sally, and several others from the cast died of cancer. The cancer rate in St. George is much higher than average. Children born there in the 1950s, according to a local pediatrician, are 2½ times more likely to contract leukemia than children born elsewhere.

St. George, whose residents are now suing the federal government, is not the only place that has been (and will be) suffering from the fallout of fear. John W. Gofman, a physician and one of the nation's most experienced authorities on the effects of radiation, has calculated from reliable data that "approximately 116,000 lung cancer deaths will occur in the United States and one million in the Northern Hemisphere as a result of weapons-testing plutonium fallout." One *million* deaths. If Dr. Gofman's figures are anywhere near correct, this is more loss of life than all the North American combat fatalities in all the wars from 1914 to the present.

It is not a coincidence that these deaths are due to the plutonium (named after the Greek god of death) that we brought into being for the purpose of dealing death to others. Take another example. In 1967, after the riots in Detroit, President Johnson stated that we had just "been through a week which no nation should have to endure," or words to that effect. Apparently the president, like most Americans, saw no connection between the riots in American cities and the unprecedented level of bombing we had just inaugurated in Vietnam. But the connections were manifold. For example, the war occasioned an unparalleled American cynicism and disrespect toward the Vietnamese people. It was a "racist war," black observers said. How, then, could we expect to have racial harmony at home?

Fear and anger are not inert things; you cannot just hurl them into someone else's court. To express fear and hatred, you have to feel them; to carry on a relationship of fear, you have to be in a state of fear. This is why high-threat relationships are always inherently unstable: If nothing else, the threateners are always destabilizing themselves from within. Those dreadful cancer deaths are only the physical expression of this inevitable fact. There is no nation so strong that it cannot be destroyed by hate. As Saint Augustine said centuries ago, "Imagine the vanity of thinking that your enemy can do more damage to you than your enmity."

REAL VISION, REAL FUTURE

As people dream, so will they become. If you prepare for war, you get war. No arms race has ever led to a stable peace; every arms race has ended in the use of arms. The "balance of power" Athens and Sparta sought at the beginning of recorded Western history leveled Hellenic civilization, as Thucydides recorded, expressly to warn us never again to rely on so unstable a prospect for security. But leaving aside the lessons of history (as we always do) there can never be a balance of power—or balance of terror, or "parity," or mutually assured destruction, or whatever we call it—because such a relationship has no psychological reality. Mutually hostile, armed, untrusting nations never seek a balance of power; each one always seeks to *overpower* the other. As a State Department official once said to me, "The worst thing you can do in an arms race is to come in second." Parity is a pretense that leaders may or may not believe in; the real motivation—and the absurdity of the problem—is that both sides perpetually want to be superior.

A universal characteristic of this world-consuming dilemma is that all parties claim and perhaps believe, eventually, that they have no choice. The continuation of nuclear weapons tests by the French put the Soviet Union in a situation that, said Ambassador Tsarapkin, "may compel it to resume atomic and hydrogen bomb tests." As the Soviets become stronger "we have no real choice" but to try to "restore our ability to deter them," NATO will "have no choice" but to increase its military build-up to correspond to the Warsaw Pact military build-up, and so on.

Is it that we have no choice, or rather that we have made the wrong basic choice already? We "decided" (if that is the right word) that the U.S.S.R. and the United States are enemies. Confusion, gobbledegook, immaturity, and a sense of paralysis inevitably follow. Starting from that position all perceptible choices are already made: Whenever there is an "enemy" or a relationship of competition, only one choice is possible, and that choice is to win.

If we want to make real choices, if we want options that don't conceal a death-dealing fallout on ourselves and trap us in a hall of mirrors where nothing we seem to do can make things better, we must get down to that basic wrong decision. We have to change what Emerson would call that "master idea reigning in the minds of many persons": East *versus* West, Soviets against Americans, us against them.

After all, what is this competition between the United States and the U.S.S.R. about? We are not locked in a deadly struggle for material resources: We sell the Soviets wheat, high technology, everything but military secrets. For the past ten years, American systems designers have helped to plan the Soviet economy. More English language books are sold each year in the Soviet Union than in the United States. And where any real military defense system might be concerned, both sides passed the "overkill" mark years ago without slowing down for an instant. Richard Barnet explains it this way:

> It is difficult to see where the military technology race could make much difference to the outcome of any plausible U.S.–Soviet conflict, given the high state of technology and the enormous armament levels on both sides. . . . The strongest incentive to stay ahead or catch up in the armaments race is prestige. . . . Being on the frontier of technology is more impressive a symbol than massive standing armies.

Prestige and symbols. I can build a better missile than you can. The game of competition and enmity. It is not based on realities; it is based on a bad idea—and we can therefore change it.

I am not particularly enthusiastic about space travel, but it has served a purpose. When cosmonaut Edgar Mitchell began his report of what he had seen from far beyond the earth, the first thing he said was, "No man I know of has gone to the moon" without experiencing "instant global consciousness. Each man comes back with a feeling that he is no longer only an American citizen; he is a planetary citizen. He doesn't like the way things are and he wants to improve it."

"Russia" and "America" are not enemies; they are just collections of people. There are no communist babies or capitalist babies. There is no American air or Soviet water. We are just people, about one-eighth of the planet's human population.

What could these two great collections of people not accomplish if they would stop competing and think of themselves as co-workers moving toward a common good from different ideological positions? Mother earth has 1½ billion starving mouths to feed. We could feed them together. In 1976, for example, when the budget for American military appropriations alone was $78 billion, it would have taken an estimated $2 billion to feed all the hungry people in the entire world, an expense that we could have easily shared. If we and the Soviet Union could resolve our differences, we would be not just superpowers but world leaders. No remaining conflict in the world could not be settled by political means. We could be on our way to ending the scourge of war.

If we would stop this huge diversion of human productivity—ideas, machines, institutions—to military expenditures, which are plainly and simply expenditures for death, and take up the job of ending worldwide poverty and starvation, the population increases of the poorest nations would taper off. Overpopulation is a result of poverty, not vice versa. People stop producing a lot of children when, as in the developed countries, they are reasonably sure some of their children will live.

If the world's peoples were not divided into military units hungry for power, the hysterical struggle for energy and technological power—also dominated by prestige and symbols rather than material needs—would subside and global development could follow a smoother, safer, more natural and equitable course. What is most important of all, an entire generation of young people all over the world would be able to look to a real future with inspiring challenges and a meaningful role to play in it.

Given this one change of "master idea," from enmity to cooperation, those who have so far been caught in the game would suddenly see possibilities in situations that appear hopeless. We, for example, would understand that the Soviets lost 20 million people in World War II, the third massive invasion they had sustained from Western Europe. After that war the Soviet Union was a physically devastated country, all but encircled by nations that did not like it and were flouting a competing ideology. Their arch enemies, ideologically, had invented a super-weapon and shown their willingness to use it on populated cities (and, as recently released documents reveal, threatened to use it on Soviet cities too).

This perception would open a new range of possibilities in our relationship with that embattled country. "It is impossible to threaten or coerce the Soviet Government," said John Nevin Sayre even before the war, "but possibly it can be won to sanity and mercy by friendly treatment and the lessening of its fears."

In June of 1963 President Kennedy delivered an extraordinary speech, which he himself had drafted, at the American University in Washington. In it he referred to the Russians as human beings and mentioned their bravery and suffering during the war, breaking a long-standing taboo against that truth. The effect on Soviet citizens was "electrifying," writes Richard Barnet: "For months some carried clippings of it in their wallets." This was the beginning of détente. But détente has not prevailed, partly because of the steady escalation of violence in American society, which has made it impossible for us to leap the gulf to a new "master idea" by which relationships other than rivalry can be contemplated and realized. Our leaders still are "like chess players in the dark," as Barnet puts it, "absorbed in a game they can barely see." But if the master idea can be changed in the minds of enough people—ordinary citizens, Pentagon lobbyists, Kremlin strategists—they will suddenly see not only the game but what lies beyond it.

Every year in *World Military and Social Expenditures*, Ruth Leger Sivard describes the human benefit that could be secured with 5 percent of the money spent that year on deadly armaments, including food for 60 million pregnant and nursing mothers, for 200 million children, safe water for all within the decade, a global program to wipe out malaria, an international campaign to secure clean air for all, research and development of labor-intensive, low-cost safe technology, and development of literacy, health care, and training programs for the young and unemployable. UN Secretary General Kurt Waldheim has proposed that nations set aside not 5 percent but 1/10 of 1 percent of their arms expenditures to be used in developing a training program and other research facilities for peace. Why even so much? asked Christian Bye at a recent European disarmament symposium; think what we would be able to do with even 1/100 of 1 percent of that vast expenditure. Yet no amount is ever set aside—not 5 percent, not 1/10 of 1 percent, not 1/100 of a percent. None of the several hundred disarmament scenarios published in the *Bulletin of Peace Proposals* has been realized. We still live in the idea of enmity, where no percentage is affordable and no scenario acceptable. Suggesting different percentages and scenarios is not going to help; we must first change our national mind-set to one in which people are not enemies but people. Then *any* percentage could start us, or any plausible scenario.

THE POWER OF THE PERSON

It is terribly difficult to pry off the grip of a pervasive master idea, especially one that has been legitimated by centuries of competitive culture and intensified by generations of crisis thinking. Which is the weakest finger? To begin, only people have ideas. Governments can influence our ideas, they can punish people with certain ideas and reward people with certain others, but only individual human beings *have* ideas, attitudes, and feelings.

Those who have tried to untangle the roots of war often forget this. Just after World War II, General Eisenhower made a memorable statement: "People want peace so badly that one day governments are going to have to step out of the way and let them have it." This is an attractive idea, that systems, governments, and institutions are the cause of war. A Soviet scholar who has worked for many years with a colleague of mine reflected recently, "Isn't the way we've been talking to one another better than the way our governments are talking to one another?" There is, as I say, much to be said for this point of view, but it happens to be an oversimplification.

Many years ago in New York City I was returning home late at night in a car with friends. As we came around a turn on the nearly empty Brooklyn freeway, our car suddenly swung to the outside lane, put on a terrific burst of speed, and careened back into position inches in front of another car. Our driver had decided that the car in front was trying to cut him off. We hadn't been paying much attention, and I don't think the driver of the other car was aware of his sudden participation in my friend's egodrama either. My friend was risking death—death for himself and everyone in both cars—just to "stay ahead" in a symbolic race that no one but he had even noticed.

I had forgotten about this episode until quite recently, when I read the following paragraphs in a letter from a paraplegic veteran of World War II:

> Having lived close to death for two years, the reasons why there is no peace seem infinitesimally flimsy. Russia wants the Dardanelles, Yugoslavia wants Trieste, the Moslems want India, labor wants more wages, capital wants more profits, *Smith wants to pass the car in front of him,* Junior wants more spending money. To these I say, is it necessary to kill and cripple human beings for these petty gains?
>
> All the troubles of the world originate in the common man. The selfish and greedy ways of nations are just the ways of each individual . . . multiplied a hundredfold. Until each of us stops "hogging the road" with his car . . . there will be no peace in the world.

I mentioned in Chapter 1 the similarity between the rash of violent episodes in the first days of the gas shortage and the president's threat to go to war for "our" oil in the Middle East. Now we can see that the similarity was much more than casual. The only secure and permanent way to disestablish the war system that funnels us toward disaster is through the minds of the individuals who more or less unconsciously create that system and then dance to its tune. Sooner or later, the impatient, selfish tendencies in people produce an impatient, selfish foreign policy—and the inevitable reaction from other nations.

Different individuals would make a different world. John Woolman once traveled deep into Indian country at a time when suspicion and hostility were sharpening between Indians and whites. He and the friends he was traveling with had settled down for the night in a rough lodge, when an agitated Indian brave appeared at the front door. Woolman at once got up to talk with him. As Woolman approached, the

Indian pulled out a tomahawk. Woolman did not shrink back. The Indian turned out to know a little English, and they talked to him, through their interpreter, until the Indian was satisfied and went off. Woolman's friends were astonished. "Though taking his hatchet in his hand at the instant I drew near to him had a disagreeable appearance," Woolman records, "I believe he had no other intent than to be in readiness in case any violence were offered to him.'"

Woolman's reaction was exactly the opposite of my friend's on the Brooklyn freeway. While my friend reacted to a conflict that was not there, Woolman assumed no conflict where there probably was. Therefore Woolman was able to head off an impending conflict, contributing slightly to improved racial relations; my friend very nearly ended things for all of us.

What we most need to cross the gulf between our prevailing "master idea" of conflict and a safer world view is a glimpse of the other bank—a vision of the world without deadly rivalry. Next we need knowledge of the mechanisms by which we could realistically get there; and finally we need, of course, the will to break out of our technological deathtrap. Vision, knowledge, and will are exclusively the properties of human individuals. Institutions can foster these properties, but in the end it is individuals who operate even these institutions. How, then, do we make more Woolmans?

In part—and this is a great advantage—we only need to stop unmaking them. At the end of the 1970s a questionnaire was given to students in grades ten through twelve, asking them what the word "nuclear" brought to mind. One of them answered, "Danger, death, sadness . . . a terrible, terrible devaluing of human life." Said a second, "It makes you wonder about how anyone could even dare to hurt others so badly." In response to other questions they replied, "I sincerely hope that we stay on good terms with the USSR" and the danger of nuclear war "has shown me how stupid some adults can be."

Yes, by the time they are ready to assume citizenship in a modern state, some adults—most adults, it seems—will be acting as if they had no choice but to follow a path uncovered at the lowest level of human aspiration. They will act politically as though they had neither con-science nor responsibility. Perhaps after a person sees 20,000 acts of violence on television, it is difficult for conscience to stay alive; perhaps after sitting through 200,000 commercials, many of them for harmful products, the responsibility one naturally feels for one's fellows is deadened. Perhaps there are other reasons, too. But for whatever reasons, most adults will not be able to act with the sensitivity, the alertness, the awareness of the future that they exhibited when they were younger and did not have the right to vote.

I met one such adult at a Thanksgiving dinner in Berkeley years ago. Our opposite political views somehow came up, and we erupted into a roaring argument in front of all the other guests. I proved the better arguer and "won," whatever that means. As we sat down to the cold, no longer very festive dinner, he concluded, "Well, you may be right. But I'm not going to change until I see 1 million people to the left of me and 1 million people to the right of me all changing first." From this I learned how useful it is to "win" a political argument. But I also glimpsed why it is that the average individual is so ineffectual and the collective unwisdom so overpowering. It is because he or she is not really acting as an individual. Somehow when we enter the collective we leave our conscience and responsibility, not to mention our powers to judge, behind—as if the collective will perform those functions for us.

It doesn't, of course. It can't. Instead, the system and the collective suffer the loss of these capacities, and so do we. Conscience and responsibility are not merely inhibitors to warn us from doing something wrong; they are dimensions of our participation in the unity of life, our awareness of one another. The only way that an individual can truly enter a collective is by expanding these capacities, not surrendering them. As Gandhi saw it, "The individual serves the family, the family serves the village," and so on, out to the largest, "oceanic circle." We serve others but obey only our own conscience. Otherwise rote obedience to the war system (a system that reflects our own unhealthiest desires) must result: In the words of Lieutenant Calley, who ordered the massacre of men, women, and children at My Lai, "I'll do as I'm told to. I'll put the American people above my own conscience, always."

Individuals who can revivify their conscience and responsibility become the regenerators of society. When Gandhi came back to India in 1915 it was a totally defeated nation. When he passed from the scene in 1948 India was a waking giant, and colonialism lay dying at its feet. That was done by one man. And *all* individuals have these capacities latent within them, regardless of how or what society has done to discourage them or how far the individual has gone to keep them out of action. After the events at My Lai had become a cause of public outcry and the full nature of what he had done bore in on him, Lieutenant Calley himself said that if he were asked to do such a thing again he would reply,"It's illegal, and I can't be a part of it."

Helen Caldicott was an ordinary person. She was a pediatrician in Melbourne, Australia, with three young children of her own. That was in the early 1960s, when the effects of ionizing radiation were just becoming generally known. Children appeared at rallies with placards saying "Score: Strontium 90, Humanity Zero." And France was testing atomic bombs in the atmosphere in Australia's back yard. Dr. Caldicott had no position in the government. She was not particularly wealthy or influential. But she *stopped* the French government from atmospheric testing. Every time it exploded a bomb, she went on television to explain what it was doing to Australian children. Soon a group of concerned women and men had gathered around her effort. They tried to confront the French government directly, without success, and had many other apparent failures. But eventually it occurred to them to take their case before an international court of law, and there they won. Today Dr. Caldicott is the driving force behind two important international peace movements, Physicians for Social Responsibility and Women for Survival.

Let's look at another case, one that in a way is even more instructive. The early 1950s were a period of great abundance for this country. Mountains of potatoes were being doused with gasoline and burned; thousands of gallons of milk were being dumped in the rivers, to "help our economy." But the population of China, in the aftermath of colonialism and a violent revolution, was on the verge of famine. One winter, while thousands of Chinese were starving and mountains of American food were wasting, one American got a bright idea. Why not send our surplus food to them? Whoever it was soon convinced the American Friends Service Committee, a Quaker organization, to make up miniature burlap sacks with labels to be sent to representatives in Congress. The labels carried a quotation from Isaiah—"If thine enemy hunger, feed him"—and the suggestion that surplus food be sent to China.

There was no response. And America and China stayed enemies, down to the debacle of Vietnam. To all appearances the idea had failed. But over twenty years later a bit of information leaked out: Back then, President Eisenhower had been in a conference with his Joint Chiefs of Staff debating the advisability of bombing mainland China as a way out of the Korean war. When the pro-bombing faction was starting to prevail, he took it in his head to send out an aide and inquire how many of those little bags had come in. The aide came back and told him it was 45,000. The president said, "Well, if 45,000 people want us to feed the Chinese, this is hardly the time to start bombing them!"

How did these efforts succeed? In the Eisenhower case, history has neglected to record the name of the person who had such a momentous and unexpected impact on the course of history. The name hardly matters. Nor does it matter that the bag people didn't "win" their campaign or find out until two decades later what they *had* accomplished. What matters is that they acted out of the "right place," and they made things better. It is not a coincidence that Dr. Caldicott's two organizations are for doctors and for women, for these tap two great sources of concern within herself, these healing and nurturing roles of the physician and the mother. And that is what matters: to awaken the forces of conscience and responsibility within ourselves—the uniting power of love.

Can others of us be awakened like this? Of course we can. Many are. The very darkness is an advantage that can help us do so. For technology has enormously increased our ability to express anger and fear, and when these forces are expressed on a broader scale, they become far more obvious. The sight of what had been a human city reduced to rubble, or of a child burned by napalm, reveals to us what war really is, as the sight of dashing dragoons engaged in swordplay never did. And there is something else. The American Civil War was one of the bloodiest in human history—for the combatants. Eight out of ten soldiers became casualties, and the recovery rate for the wounded was very poor. But outside of some incidents such as the burning of Atlanta, not many noncombatants were directly hurt. Time has changed all that. On the accompanying graph (Fig. 3), you can see how the percentage of direct civilian casualties has steadily increased with the introduction of civilian bombing and other inevitable changes in the character of war.

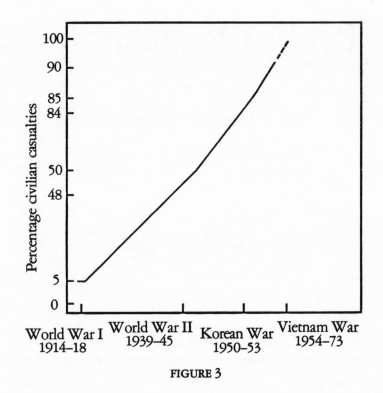

FIGURE 3

Now the war we face—if mutual annihilation is a war—would cut such a swath from life that the soldier under arms would hardly be worse off than the civilian sitting in his or her living room wishing for peace. The crisis is not merely in the tension between the United States and the U.S.S.R.; it has become a crisis of war itself. We are all involved. Each of us is its potential victim. Should someone else do the work to end it?

8|Right Occupation

The most important missing ingredient for creating an appropriate security system is the willingness of ordinary people to work with determination and tireless dedication.

Robert C. Johansen

Those who drive out anger and fear do the highest work in the world.

Buddha

We cannot begin to create a world that does not continually produce warfare and other forms of violence without reconsidering the idea of human work. At present, half a million highly trained engineers and scientists all over the world are working on military research and development. In highly concentrated military-industrial areas, the Santa Clara Valley of California, for example, such high percentages of human effort are organized to produce military equipment that regional economies are locked into these capital-intensive, humanly destructive manufactures. But the problem goes somewhat deeper. If people do not have something satisfactory to do, their frustration can lead to violence in myriad forms.

One pathway to this result is that unemployment causes a certain amount of crime by setting people adrift and in need of money; other pathways are less obvious, and more important. Since the Industrial Revolution the logic of work in the West has "progressed" from using people as machines—"flesh machines," as Kropotkin called them—to not using them at all. Today, in fact, we seem to be on the verge of a new era of technology-based unemployment: the era of the micro chip, which has already idled hundreds of thousands of skilled workers worldwide. It is good for actual machines to take some of the drudgery out of human effort, but not for them to replace that effort. The

122

changeover from working people as machines to working machines instead of people was inevitable but unsatisfactory. True progress requires us to develop a system that puts people to work *as people*.

It is no coincidence that a major part of Gandhi's freedom struggle lay in putting millions of Indian villagers who had been idled by the British-imposed economic system back to work. Danilo Dolci, sometimes called the "Sicilian Gandhi" for his work of reconstructing peasant society in that heavily terrorized and exploited region, made his greatest impact by organizing a "strike in reverse," in which the men and women of a township rebuilt their own road in defiance of governmental (and Mafia) authority. Part of the way to peace must be a way to put the human spirit back to work.

ON SPIRITUAL EMPLOYMENT

Imagine that you were in the town of Chartres around the turn of the thirteenth century, interviewing the stonemasons who were then at work on the great cathedral. If you asked them what they were doing, one worker might answer, "I'm here making a living." A second might say, "I am dressing a stone." And a third might tell you, "I am building a cathedral." If questioned, most of us today, whatever our livelihoods, would probably have to answer with the first worker. Now that even educators have come to feel that their primary role is to train students to "make a living," it is difficult to find people who know why they are working or what they are doing beyond collecting wages. Money takes the place of more and more values, with unforeseen harmful consequences everywhere. "The various causes of the loss of farmland," says political journalist Peter Ognibene of one of the nation's most serious economic problems, "can be distilled into a single word: money."

There is nothing wrong with earning money; it's just that as a criterion for the value of human work, it is totally inadequate. If it were adequate, we could look to, for example, the Detroit assembly line, that still-classic example of a modern industrial occupation, for a model of all that is desirable. But the Detroit assembly line, which has remained essentially unchanged since it was so bitterly satirized by Charlie Chaplin in *Modern Times*, is a drastically unsatisfactory place for a human being to work. "Unless you've been on the line," a former assembler said, "you can't begin to imagine the unrelieved monotony of that kind of work." It pushes you to the point where "you've got to have a release."

Bad things happen to people who have been in such a state too long. Often they take to looking for excitement, not infrequently in forms of violence. In Sweden, auto assemblers work together in groups, and each group takes responsibility for the complete assembly of a car, dividing up tasks as group members see fit by group discussion. Thus in Sweden workers work on an *automobile*, not on a left front door window or one bolt of a transmission housing. More importantly, the workers interact with their colleagues, making decisions with them, cooperating, maybe rubbing off some of the angles and corners of their personalities as they would in other aspects of everyday social life. I have heard somewhere that an American firm interested in these human improvements for its workers, and also in the fact that the Swedish assemblers were much more efficient, sent a team over to Uppsala to learn about this work style. But the American team said, "No, thanks, we're not interested," and came back to the fifty-week grind and dreams of a two-week vacation in Las Vegas. After a while, what with all the other disorienting influences in life today, workers internalize their exploitation. Even when offered the opportunity, sometimes they have already lost the desire for work that is interesting, challenging, and humane.

At bottom the trouble with the kind of work epitomized by the assembly line is that it is meaningless. Money does not provide a reason why automobiles should be manufactured without regard to what they do to the environment, or to the fossil fuel reserves, or to the temptations they put in the way of teenagers. Nor does it provide a reason for standing at the line and assembling them. Lack of meaning is conspicuous in many other areas of modern work, particularly that of the large corporations. That becomes clear when you try to write advertising copy to sell their "images." Recently David Ogilvy of Ogilvy and Mather Advertising Agency said to members of the Dallas Advertising League, "In the course of defining the purpose of your corporate advertising, it is often necessary to define the purpose of the corporation, and—you know this—most corporations do not have any purpose."

Work without purpose creates the strong sense of life without purpose; and life without purpose is a fertile breeding ground for violence: "No job, wasn't getting nowhere, having one party after another, and I had to start thinking about my future. So I joined the

Army infantry to finish high school and get some muscles. And it'll give me some money to buy a motorcycle."

For a society to be healthy, it must give people meaningful work. Otherwise, like the men on the assembly lines, who talk incessantly of sex and deer hunting, or like the seventeen-year-old boy just quoted, or those criminals of whom psychologist Stanton Samenow says, "Excitement is the oxygen of their lives," they are almost bound to drift into violence one way or another.

Full employment is a goal few contemporary societies seem able to reach. Governments rise and fall on their ability to tinker with the system and get us closer to it by a few percent. Yet full employment is always interpreted statistically. It should also, more importantly, be spiritually interpreted. Governments should be judged on their ability to give people full spiritual employment: work that uses not just their bodies, not just their technical skills, does not just harness their brains in "think tanks," but uses the full human being *as* a human being—conscious, responsible, creative. Full employment is employment of body, mind, and spirit.

WITHOUT A VISION

"Without a vision," reads Proverbs 29:18, "the people perish." Jung, Toynbee, Spengler, Einstein, and innumerable intellectual giants of our civilization have affirmed that human life is not human unless we have some sense of an overriding purpose. And we have all felt this. As Simone de Beauvoir records in her autobiography, "I cannot reconcile myself to living if there is no purpose in my life."

Making money is not a purpose. It just does not answer to that need, no matter how much people make do with it. A historian and useful commentator on our times, Theodore Roszak, reminds us that beneath the bustle of modern civilization lies an obvious truth that cannot remain hidden: "Power and possessions are without significance for the whole and healthy person. They become goals only by default and to the degree that higher purpose withdraws from our lives."

One of the most important thinkers on the purpose of human life—important because he has made such dramatic practical use of his discoveries—is the Viennese psychiatrist Viktor Frankl. Out of the crucible of his ghastly experiences in the concentration camps of World

War II came his awareness that the "striving to find a meaning in one's life is the primary motivational force in man." This fact distinguishes human beings from their evolutionary forebears, and it must be reckoned with in the treatment of psychiatric disorders, the prevention of crime, the rehabilitation of criminals (where respect for meaning in life and the individual's own responsibility have created the few success stories in an otherwise drifting and beleaguered profession), and other aspects of social policy. In a well-controlled experiment at a convalescent hospital outside Boston, all the patients were given house plants. One half were told to water and care for the plants themselves, and the other half that the nurses would look after the plants for them. The recovery rate for the group that was given this minimal responsibility for a living thing was twice that of the other group.

Frankl is clearly right in saying that what we human beings need is not some sort of happy homeostasis in which all our wants are satisfied but "the striving and struggling for some goal worthy of [us]." But Frankl takes another important step. He cautions us against casually fixing on a purpose for our lives, because life has a purpose, and our task is not to invent one—a ready temptation in the modern world—but to discover it. "We had to teach the despairing men," he found, "that *it did not really matter what we expected from life, but rather what life expected from us.*" And what does life expect from us? The universal yearning in every human being for spiritual unity and peace is our clearest answer.

Work, then, has many purposes besides supplying us with an individual livelihood. In ancient Greek, *tīmē*, meaning "work," "office," "responsibility," also meant "honor," "value," "worth." A man or woman with a sense of purpose will suffer if he or she does not have something significant to do, while someone in whom this sense is dormant will fight shy of work that is tinged with idealism. Conversely, people who are given important work to do will come to feel important, while people who are idled, no matter how much money or other tokens of esteem they are loaded with, will not be able to shake off a haunting sense of worthlessness. Unemployment causes crime not so much because it causes poverty but because having nothing to do depletes our sense of self-worth and, from there, our sense of the value and dignity of life.

In recent years, no one has thought more about this issue or shed more light on the significance of work than the great economist E. F. Schumacher. "It has been recognized," he writes, "in all authentic teachings of mankind that every human being born into this world has to work not merely to keep himself alive but to strive towards perfection." "To keep himself alive," he continues,

> he needs various goods and services which will not be forthcoming without human labour. To perfect himself, he needs purposeful activity in accordance with the injunction: "Whichever gift each of you have received, use it in service to one another, like good stewards dispensing the grace of God in its varied forms." From this, we may derive the three purposes of human work as follows:
>
> > First, to provide necessary and useful goods and services; second, to enable everyone of us to use and thereby to perfect our gifts like good stewards; and third, to do so in service to, and in cooperation with, others so as to liberate ourselves from our inborn egocentricity.

Measured by the standard of these purposes so well expressed by Schumacher, the work of the modern assembly plant or factory is hugely defective. So many manufactured goods are unnecessary, so many are harmful. Assembling micro chips under government contracts in Santa Clara may be enjoyable or lucrative, but no number of euphemisms such as "defense" or "lethal *aid*" conceals the fact that the majority of this equipment has as its most direct purpose the killing and maiming of human beings. The automobile, although not necessarily a lethal weapon, is looking less and less like a "necessary and useful good."

Still less do the conditions of the modern factory or, for that matter, of the modern office, where employees also may be treated as cogs in a money-making system, encourage workers to develop their full talents or liberate themselves from inborn egocentricity. A famous study by social scientists from the University of Oklahoma strongly confirms Schumacher's contention that working together has this power to overcome egocentricity and conflict. Groups of boys at a summer camp who had been badly polarized by competitive games and other devices were quickly reunited not by watching movies or by playing games together but by cooperating actively on common tasks, or "superordinate goals," as the scientists called them, like repairing a truck that both groups needed or cleaning up the camp's common water supply. The Swedish factory style we mentioned earlier is an attempt to build this kind of cooperation into the structure of the assembly plant. Most offices and factories, however, aren't interested; there the work goals—the profits of the firm—are too distant from the worker and her or his cooperation with other workers too mechanical for that liberating process to take place.

Many immemorial human occupations that took all three of these important purposes into account are not surviving the advances of industrialization. Around the turn of the century one-third of the population of the United States lived on small farms. By 1969, only one-twentieth were still there, and the number dwindles rapidly. Since 1940 more than 25 million Americans have left the family farm, and to some degree the important values that it nurtured and represented. The family farm was an important social institution. Its decline—not to mention the decline of the family—has had repercussions far beyond economic ones. (In fact, the economic repercussions turned out to be the reverse of what our strange fascination with bigness and centralization led us to expect: Family farms are more productive per unit of land under cultivation than agribusinesses.) Our sense of stewardship for the land is also being destroyed. As 200,000 to 400,000 farms go under every year, twelve square miles of fertile farmland every *day* get turned into "real estate," or go to ruin, falling under the condominium or the parking lot instead of the plow, or wash away into the nation's rivers because we have lost sight of what the land means. As far as America's responsibility to the rest of the world is concerned, some agricultural specialists fear that disasters lie ahead because of this loss, some of it irreversible, of American farmlands. We are one of the world's most important sources of food.

Another kind of farming that has been made over in the image of mass production, with particularly unfortunate consequences, is animal raising. Economically, the transformation is ill-advised, since animal foods are an enormously inefficient way to get protein from grain. Physically, it jeopardizes our health, since these foods are high in cholesterol and chemical pollutants. Spiritually, we are compromised in various ways: Soybeans and grains that could be saving people from death are going to feed enormous numbers of hogs and cattle for our tables. But this isn't the whole story. Recently in my part of the country a large operation that was breaking up sent around an auction catalogue that included among the "objects" that were up for sale—cars, tractors, typewriters, and adding machines—one Black Angus steer. "Free slaughtering" could be thrown in, the catalogue said.

Many of us might think the institution of the "sacred cow" in India, or other customs like it, irrational. We forget that such customs and institutions have a purpose. It makes economic sense not to slaughter cows in India (you can get milk from your living cow a lot longer than you can get meat from your dead cow). Even more importantly, this unwillingness to kill sets up a *relationship* people have with the cow, and through her with all animals—a relationship of real psychological value and real survival value, as any relationship has that helps us to conquer alienation and work in harmony with the unity of life. By contrast, our exploitative attitude toward the animals nature has put in our power (or was it in our care?) has produced not only, as I say, bad economics but also bad relationships with this part of our world. A farmer friend of mine confided that "keeping sows tied down or penned alone all their lives is . . . a substitute for good husbandry, for humane stewardship. . . . The by-product is cruelty and the motive is profit." The production of food is a sacred trust, a responsibility that forms part of our individual and social purpose. The greed that made us turn food into a business (or a weapon) has dehumanized our lives in ways we might never have predicted.

Human happiness is an elusive thing. George Bernard Shaw was once asked if he was happy and he replied, very wisely, that he must be, because he never gave it a moment's thought. In this sense, happiness is like security. If we try to grab security directly, more often than not we only push it away. But we can be secure indirectly, by living in such a way that we avoid making enemies and resolve our differences with the enemies we do make. We can be secure by contributing to the security of others. And we can be happy indirectly, by contributing to the happiness of others. Einstein's friends said that he had a "total inability to despair," that most characteristic ailment of modern times. And his own prescription was, "Always order your life around a central goal." Einstein took his pad and pencil with him to the hospital and was working practically up to the moment that he died. He exemplified

Saint Thomas Aquinas's dictum: "There can be no joy of life without joy of work."

MAKING THE BREAK WITH VIOLENCE

In the preceding sections we have seen: that human beings need full employment if they are to live in a way that no longer leads to violence; that full employment means the use of all our superb human gifts–of body, mind, and spirit; that spiritual employment means employment with an overriding purpose; and that purpose means something conducive to the unity of life. Work that produces harm is obviously not spiritual employment or what the Buddha would call "right occupation," whether the harmful product is cigarettes or bullets. Other cases may be much less obvious. As Schumacher puts it, our work must give us a way of serving the well-being of others and reducing our "inborn egocentricity," because that is a direct contribution to human unity. We do this, as he outlines, both by cooperating with others *in* our work and by serving others *by* our work–in other words, by getting involved in the evolution of human unity both according to the short-range and the long-range consequences of our efforts. No amount of camaraderie on the job will enable us to develop fully if our "job" is designing missiles; on the other hand, our development will be stunted even by making bandages for the Red Cross if we make them in our garrets, snarling at anyone who tries to help.

From society's point of view, providing work that is not harmful, that is, ideally, helpful, and that is conducive to working in a good spirit is the way to guarantee society's health. From the individual's point of view, however, it is idle to wait for society to provide us with full spiritual employment. Making our work be what it should is part of the work itself. Let's look at some people who have done this.

My friend Bob Farmer is quiet, with a soft Texas drawl and an unassertive manner. It doesn't take long, though, to start responding to the liveliness of his eyes and appreciating the determined way he sets about to do things. In his way, Bob might be one of the last Texas pioneers. Eighteen years ago he left a lucrative job designing rocket control systems for an engineering firm in southern California and headed out on his own for a career in experimental medicine. This is how he explained the transformation to me:

I think people should know about this, because there are a lot of scientists who were in my position and who still are. It's an unquestioned assumption with them. They genuinely believe that what they are doing is for the best, but as you say there is an element of personal convenience in it too. I know in my case there was convenience, all right: the draft was looming over me ready to snap me up if I didn't go into war research. I was more or less forced that way, and like so many others, I began to think that way.

So I came from MIT with a master's in electrical engineering straight to _____ Astronautics in San Diego and missile systems. We were all on government money through some fund or other–good salaries, everybody had his TR3 or some nice car to drive through the big gates into the security lot, the people were nice–and of course it was right in San Diego.

It wasn't at all clear cut, how I first started to feel that there was something wrong. It had something to do with sitting around at engineers' meetings where everyone was eating sandwiches and matter-of-factly talking about the best way to destroy a city. It was all very creative, with people shooting out ideas–the advantages of multiple warheads over patterned rockets.

I don't think anyone else was inclined the way I was. In fact, when I tried to tell people close to me that I wanted to get out of the field they were very upset–uprooted. They couldn't imagine what was bothering me, and at that time I couldn't tell them very clearly myself. *This* meant a good job, security, and *that* meant . . . who knows what?

In those days Baylor was offering a summer fellowship in bioengineering, which one of my friends had interested me in back in college. That seemed to me like a way to get started. The company assured me that there was no place with them for someone with that kind of interest, so there was only one way to go, and I went–out.

My job at the medical center is just about ideal for me now. My dissertation on cell physiology, however interesting, had lacked a sense of usefulness, but now the patients are right there, lining the halls, and boy does that give you motivation!

What I did should never be called a switch, actually; it should be called a maturing and developing experience. You learn physiology but you don't forget engineering–you put it all together and come out with something you can *use*, something that really makes sense for people's welfare.

You know, when I was back at MIT we studied "control systems." Nobody told us they could be used to guide rockets loaded with nuclear warheads; nobody ever asked us to think about what we were doing. I wish people in the business of weapons research could realize that there is a much more fulfilling occupation.

"Something that really makes sense for people's welfare." That idea crops up again and again in the words of people like Bob Farmer; like Robert Aldridge, who walked out on his top-level work designing the

Trident submarine (when he realized it was part of a first strike policy) and founded an important policy research institute; like the three engineers from GE who resigned and started a consulting firm to translate nuclear gobbledegook into plain English for firms or governments that want to understand what the nuclear industry is actually saying; and like a growing band of individuals who are leaving war industry in Silicon Valley (the area around Santa Clara, California) and elsewhere all over the world for the very same reason—"to work on products which actually help to solve human problems rather than create them."

Twenty-five percent of the nation's defense contracts and one-third of its military research and development are concentrated in the Silicon Valley. Here the Mid-Peninsula Conversion Project has set up shop to explain to management, workers, and members of the surrounding communities how much better economic sense and better common sense it would make if industry produced components for public transportation instead of tanks, solar collectors instead of rockets, heart pacers instead of reentry systems and superspy equipment.

The project's newspaper, a bimonthly called the *Plowshare Press*, carries little-known studies that reveal how all but 6 of 127 skills in use at a particular weapons plant could be turned toward useful products without retraining the workers, how 19,000 highly skilled, unemployed aerospace workers in Santa Clara County could have been working in the environment or in education (if the government would transfer some of its defense allocation to the school system), how the Solar Energy Industries Association could have provided 11 million American homes (15 percent) solar systems by 1985 had they been supported. It explains with facts and figures how wasteful and unreliable military industry is—the $1.4 billion on a missile project that was known to have no earthly use, the wild fluctuations in hiring and firing as contracts come and go—not to mention how destructive it is to our security and morale. It points out the dangers of nuclear technology, how the nation nonetheless spent $1.7 billion to research and develop it in 1978 alone, compared to the pittance it devotes to solar energy. It carried a quote from an anonymous engineer who explained why he "dropped out" of defense work:

> During the last several years at _____ I have realized that high technology is very expensive. I feel that if my tax dollars are going to be used

> for very expensive research, I would rather have the research done in a more positive area, directly *helping people to have a better life.*

Plowshare Press exposes its readers to the ideas of Schumacher and Gandhi, who are passed over by our "no choice," supply-side economists. And it reports regularly on the progress of the Lucas Aerospace workers conversion plan.

This plan, a 2,500-page document, was drawn up by the shop stewards of Lucas, the largest military contractor in Britain, and presented to the board of directors in 1976. The plan outlines a conversion of the seventeen plants and 80,000 workers "from military production to meeting the needs of people." A revised "corporate plan" of 350 pages, calling for, among other things, the workers at the factory in Burnley to be allowed to produce the combined diesel-electric bus they designed themselves, has recently been recognized by the management and the then–British minister for industry, Gerald Kaufman. It is not only "the first time in industrial history that any company has sat down with the unions to come up with an alternative to unemployment" (one-third of Lucas's aerospace workers had been laid off since 1970); it is also a milestone in the conversion or, as the French accurately call it, the "reconversion" of industry to meaningful and satisfying work.

The challenges of conversion transcend national boundaries. Workers in France, Belgium, West Germany, and many other countries have been taking up this program of breaking our dependence on military manufactures, that wrong occupation that gives reliable jobs to so few and meaningful work to none. The issue, according to Douglas Mattern of the World Citizens' Assembly, is nothing less than "transforming our societies to new values and purposes"; or in the words of an American machinist: "Somebody in this country has got to change what we do for a living. We have the greatest concentration of minds and skills. We have the freedom to develop what we wish. [Yet] we are . . . selling arms to whoever has the money." And we are all, of course, the "somebodies" in question.

SELF-EMPLOYMENT

Militarism is the most spectacular, but not the only form of violence, and military industry is not the only work situation that needs changing. Nelson Shields was a successful executive with Du Pont in

1974, when his son fell victim to the "Zebra" murderer in San Francisco. Suddenly it seemed meaningless to him to be working for private ends in the face of the dissolution of civilization. Du Pont is not a military firm; it manufactures some useful products and some harmful ones, wherever profit seems to lead it. But Shields could no longer reconcile himself to working for "money, prestige, and the good life" in times of such dire need. He started spending weekends in Washington helping the gun control lobby, and when he felt the time was right he gave up his position at Du Pont and became chairman of the National Council to Control Handguns, at one-fourth his previous salary.

Many people have been undone or embittered by senseless, personal tragedies. But for Shields it was the beginning of something not so senseless, and much more than personal. As he puts it, "Maybe my son's death was the good Lord's way of turning my life to more productive paths." His response was to "do everything in [his] power to reduce the probability of someone else's son suffering the same fate." These remarks are extremely important because they show precisely the qualities that help us learn from experience: a sense of overriding purpose and a sense that one's own life is not unconnected with the whole. The message for the rest of us is not to wait to find meaningful work until violence strikes at a son, a father, or ourselves!

The ideal work to be converted *to* is work that makes a direct contribution to international peace instead of war or, as in Mr. Shields' case, to domestic peace instead of violence. Work in these fields tends to relate directly to all Schumacher's criteria. "I always had the feeling," writes Dr. Caldicott, "that our marches exemplified the way people should relate to one another, as concerned human beings working together for survival." It will be a long time before society regularly furnishes salaries for such work, and in any case the problem goes much further than the way we happen to make a living. It involves how far we should expect to go in committing ourselves to working for a better world. Perhaps the following image offers us a guideline.

Erskine Caldwell wrote *God's Little Acre* about a family in the Deep South and the widower who tries to raise that family and provide his children with some guidance. Ty Ty is a decent man. He knows that money isn't everything. He firmly believes that God can help them. So he sets aside one acre of his land, "God's little acre," and vows to give everything that acre yields to God. But the chosen acre gets in the way when they decide to dig up the place for gold, and so they move it. What does God care *which* acre it is? But no matter where they put it, God's little acre interferes with some project or other. By the end of the novel, when the family has been knocked about by fate and there is no gold and no satisfaction, God's little acre is somewhere in the outback where Ty Ty never even sees it.

I think what Caldwell was trying to say is that if you want to establish a grounding principle in your life, it's not enough just to have that principle around. It does little good to keep it on a shelf, to be remembered in emergencies. It has to be an *active* principle, not something set aside but something central in the sense that it gives meaning and direction to all other interests. Eventually there should be no competing principle or activities in our lives—this is the positive corollary to the zero strategy. Everything we do should be guided by the main idea we have chosen as our polestar.

Right occupation embraces much more than how we happen to make a living. It is everything that occupies us, it is how we live. Peace—a life without violence—will require that we work for it full time. This does not mean that we do nothing with our lives but "direct. action"—lobbying, educating, protesting for peace—but that we have a life-nurturing purpose at the center of all our activities and, to the extent that it is humanly possible, the center of our states of mind. It hardly matters whether the work is salaried. What matters is that it grows out of a *wholehearted* intention to make the world a better place, as far as in us lies. In our small ways we should be able to say, with Gandhi, "My life is an indivisible whole, and all my activities have their rise in my insatiable love of mankind."

Economies and work existed long before the paycheck, and the most important work of women and men may well be that for which society offers no monetary reward, no support, which may earn us censure or imprisonment. But if the work "makes sense for the welfare of people," it is basically right and progressive. As with the civil rights movement, it can become the legitimate cause of tomorrow.

One of the most creative actions undertaken in the recent history of nonviolence (nonviolent activists have to be high in creativity and imagination) was the campaign by Danilo Dolci I mentioned at the beginning of this chapter. Dolci has carried on a lifelong nonviolent struggle against the Mafia on the one hand and the civil authorities on the other, who between them retard Sicily's social progress and keep thousands of its inhabitants in economic stagnation (not to mention chronic insecurity). Dolci initiated his campaign when a whole region was cut off from the outside world and sources of employment by the condition of a road, and the government would not spend the money to repair it even though most of the local people were out of work. He simply organized a "strike in reverse": On an appointed day the men showed up with their picks and shovels and set about repairing their road. Dolci and many of the crew were arrested under some odd regulation, but the point was made and the strangle hold of the Mafia and the paralytic embrace of the authorities were loosened. Dolci's full-time work now encompasses schools, a social research center, the building of dams (sixteen completed to date), and hundreds on hundreds of meetings in which the local people are learning how to organize their own political and economic lives.

In our affluent and industrially "developed" society dams and roads would not have the same significance, but right purpose and grass-roots organization still do. In my locality, a small group of mothers has made an impact in their efforts to reduce the violence on television and get pornography off local newsstands where it is displayed in front of children. These women speak the classic language of nonviolence, though they may never have heard of it: "There is a good side to all people," they explain. "We appeal to that side for cooperation." Another group of women doing similar work says, "Our thrust is aimed at anything that degrades the human being."

These examples give an idea of how many things are waiting to be done once we coordinate our own purposes with the overall purpose of helping humankind toward a state of more perfect harmony and get rid of the idea that the only work available is what society pays us to do and encourages us to do.

Something also needs to be said about *how* we work, not only about what we work on. It is often forgotten that the spirit in which we undertake anything determines its quality at least as much as what that thing is.

The people who do the best work always have a sense of detachment that puzzles most of us, thinking as we do that hard work implies the kind of relentless drive we normally associate with ambition. Edison once made a curious statement: "I never worked a day in my life." He did not mean that inventing things was a lark. The proportion of perspiration to inspiration was as high there as it is in any other job. But Edison was working for a reasonably selfless purpose. Most of his inventions were in fact useful at that time, and in any case he made them largely in a spirit of serving human progress, not for his own self-aggrandizement.

Gandhi was an even more striking example. He worked into his seventies on a schedule that would kill a junior executive: fifteen or so hours a day, seven days a week, months at a time on the road, carried on for almost fifty years. Yet when John Gunther, author of *Inside U.S.A.,* asked him, "Gandhi, don't you want to take a vacation?" he shot back, "John, I'm always on vacation!" He meant that "he," as we usually think of the self-oriented human personality, had been put out to pasture a long time ago and that what he called "the greatest force man has ever been endowed with," nonviolence, was acting *through* him.

Most Indians regard such people as Gandhi or Mother Teresa with veneration. Indians feel that something divine is working through them because they have given up the personal satisfactions that are normal to most of us, which enables them to work phenomenally hard and phenomenally effectively without exhaustion; the more they work, the more they are fulfilled. For us the best explanation is perhaps that in these people—and this is a process that could be further advanced in all of us—the normal competitive, acquisitive drives have been transformed into a desire for the well-being of life as a whole. That makes for right occupation, whatever we undertake as a vehicle for that desire.

In fact, the very process of getting to that condition of being able to work on something larger-than-self with enthusiastic dedication and yet with detachment *is* right occupation. It is precisely what Einstein meant by our "task" of liberating ourselves from the prison of limited compassion. This fact has a very positive result: Useful "work" is available for everyone. Society can refuse to pay me for teaching nonviolence, but it cannot prevent me from being nonviolent. If I so much as control my temper when someone pushes me once too often on a bus, choosing instead to look for ways to make people more conscious of one another, if I restrain myself from being aggressive with the people whom I could get to do things I want by beetling my brows at them, I am "driving out anger and fear," as the Buddha said, which in a small way is my contribution to the "highest work in the world." If I begin to arrive at the consistency of which Gandhi spoke, my contribution may not even be that small.

The work I have been describing is the work we are really cut out for, and every other kind of work is moonlighting. Harvard Law Professor Roger Fisher tells an arresting story about a B-29 test flight he once was making over Newfoundland. The pilot, not quite thinking what he was doing, feathered all four propellers—forgetting that to restart them you need electric current, and for electric current aboard a B-29 you need running engines. As they glided soundlessly toward the Newfoundland rocks the copilot burst out, "Boy, do you have a problem!" But a technical sergeant who happened to be along remembered that there was an old gas-powered generator stored away in the bomb bay somewhere. While the rest of the crew members were buckling into their parachutes, he sweated and tugged and pulled at the starting cord, fired up the generator, and saved the plane. Whose responsibility was it to save the plane, asks Professor Fisher? It was that very sergeant's, of course—not because he had caused the problem, not because it was his assigned job to solve it, but because he *could*. Responsibility is defined by opportunity.

In that sense we all are responsible for doing something about war and violence—because we can. There is no unemployment. Full employment is already here, for all of us. All we need is the courage to get started.

9 | Love for All

*Therefore Love is able to attempt all things, and it
accomplishes many things, and warrants them to take
effect; where he that loves not will faint and lie down.*

Thomas à Kempis

Human intelligence being the most underdeveloped resource on
the planet, we sometimes see through a glass so darkly that the shadow
becomes the light and the light the shadow. A Los Angeles hockey
player is sent back to the farm team for *not* leaving the bench to
participate in a brawl; young men who *do* feel scruples about registering
for the draft are considered selfish; when we have a conflict with other
nations our first reaction is *not* to talk to them. And so it is with the
important phenomenon of nonviolence. The very word, "*non*violence,"
shows that we are trying to look at the phenomenon through the dark
glasses that give a reverse image of reality: We take nonviolence to be
the absence of something or its negation, not a thing but a non–something else. This distortion has marked the long history of the idea.
Adin Ballou, you recall, called it "(Christian) non-resistance" or "non-
injury." The same assumption lies behind the usage of other lan-
guages, for instance, German, in which it becomes *Gewehrlosigkeit*, "de-
fenselessness," or, still more inaccurately, *Ohnmacht*, "lack of power."
A neighbor of mine, in response to the idea that nonviolence could
be an answer to our social problems, said immediately, "But there isn't
much power in nonviolence."

AN IDEA WHOSE TIME HAS COME

As Gandhi said, "Non-violence is the greatest force man has ever
been endowed with." It is in all likelihood the most positive force in the
universe. Without it, as Kropotkin realized when he discovered the
"mutual aid factor" in evolution, all social progress would have stopped
long ago and "human society could not be maintained for even one
single generation." It is this power that we have to understand–by

turning inside out some of our preconceptions and by looking for what *is* there: not the negation of something else but the thing itself.

Here it is best to look to the people who have actually used nonviolence. One of them, of course, was George Fox. The year that Cromwell died, 1658, was one of great tribulation for Fox and the Society of Friends. "Great stirs were in the nation, the minds of the people being unsettled," and many Friends, too, were tempted to fly to arms to defend themselves or to take advantage of the chaos to advance their positions. Fox sent out a ringing epistle to warn them of the dangers of such a move and inspired them to:

> Stand in the fear and dread of the Lord God; His power, life, light, seed and wisdom, by which ye may take away the occasion of wars, and so know a kingdom which hath no end, *and fight for that with spiritual weapons*, which takes away the occasion of the carnal, and there gather men to war, as many as ye can, and set up as many as ye can with these weapons.

What exactly are "spiritual weapons"? He was simply referring to the power of love. "Love has more power," said Saint Teresa somewhere, "than a besieging army." Similarly, the Buddha described a "true brahmin" as one who "fears neither jail nor death: He has the power of love no army can defeat." But the love they are speaking of is rather different from the love we speak of when we describe, for example, the love of one person for another, which is a wonderful thing, but which has never prevailed against the power of wars. The love that Fox, Saint Teresa, and others are alluding to is love for *all*. It is the commitment to expand our circles of compassion outward without limit. It starts as the love we are familiar with but becomes qualitatively different: This kind of love makes us unsatisfied to love only this person or another; it means we cannot bear the alienation of being for one party against another, as though we were divided against ourselves. When we think of loving the people in an oppressed country whom we have never seen—and their oppressors!—we realize that this love requires an immense unification of individual drives and predilections and could well generate within us a greater than individual force. "My life is an indivisible whole," said Gandhi, and "all of my actions have their rise in my insatiable love of mankind."

One example of how this kind of love can work comes from an

eyewitness account of a great civil rights breakthrough that occurred in Birmingham, Alabama, in 1964. That was the year a major civil rights march found its way blocked by the city's police and firemen. Everything Martin Luther King and his followers had worked for was put to the test in this confrontation, and this is what happened:

> "We're going to win our freedom," a Negro leader said at a mass meeting in Birmingham last year, "and as we do it we're going to set our white brothers free." A short while later, when the Negroes faced a barricade of police dogs, clubs and fire hoses, they "became spiritually intoxicated," as another leader described it. "This was sensed by the police and firemen and it began to have an effect on them. . . . I don't know what happened to me. . . . I got up from my knees and said to the cops: 'We're not turning back. We haven't done anything wrong. All we want is our freedom. How do you feel doing these things?'" The Negroes started advancing and Sheriff Bull Connor shouted: "Turn on the water!" But the firemen did not respond. Again he gave the order and nothing happened. Some observers claim that they saw firemen crying. Whatever happened, the Negroes went through the lines. . . . Until now this mood of outgoing empathetic nonviolence has been rarely achieved in this country. It was only part of the story in Birmingham, where in the end a more cautious tokenism gripped the top leaders. But it is the clue to the potential power of nonviolence.

This is not an isolated occurrence in the annals of nonviolence. British police fell back before a slowly advancing band of unarmed demonstrators crossing a field in India because even when the latter were beaten to the ground they stood up and kept advancing with smiles on their faces. "You just can't hit a chap who smiles at you like that," the police would say later.

The force of this love, as Martin Luther King said, is "passive physically, but strongly active spiritually"; that is, "while the nonviolent resister is passive in the sense that he is not physically aggressive toward his opponent, his mind and his emotions are constantly active," constantly seeking to persuade the opposition. These "spiritual weapons" do what guns and armies only pretend to do—they defend us. What is more, as the examples quoted above show, they can bring about the kind of great social changes on which stability and true security depend.

Although they can be used for social changes, these "spiritual weapons" do not arise from society. As we have seen before, they are brought into play when the individual contacts more love for all within.

Then it can radiate outward as a social force; it can even restructure international relations—but it can only arise from the individual who learns to use it first in his or her most intimate relationships. I once had occasion to present a book on Gandhi to the former prime minister of India, Morarji Desai. By chance he opened it to a full-page picture of Gandhi's wife. "Kasturba!" said the prime minister. "You know, he learned nonviolence from *her*." Gandhi's autobiography leaves no doubt that he became a mahatma not in the great campaigns for the rights of indentured Indians in South Africa but right at home with Kasturba. If the battle of Waterloo was won on the playing fields of Eton, as in a sense it was, the independence of India was won in the tempestuous Gandhi living room.

Love—that great liberating force for change—is the positive of which violence is the negation. We may be coming closer to understanding this. One of the German expressions newly coined to grapple with the concept of nonviolence, and an improvement on the others, is *Gewalt-freiheit*—"freedom from violence."

This freedom and the power behind it, everything denoted by the concept of nonviolence, is indeed, as it is often called nowadays, "an idea whose time has come." We must see to it, however, that it does come, and on time. It is urgent, then, to ask, what kind of force is this nonviolence, how does it work, and—most importantly—how can we learn to use it?

A LIVING FORCE

Gandhi always insisted that he had not invented anything, that there was no such thing as "Gandhism," and that truth and nonviolence were as "old as the hills." He was just a scientist, an experimenter; what he experimented with was the truth and what he discovered was its practical application, love for all. The problem is that although truth, love, and nonviolence are as "old as the hills," although they have been silently at work in the life process since before there were *Homo sapiens*, we human beings on the whole are at a primitive stage of understanding and developing them.

The tinkerers who preceded Gandhi, the Marconis and Edisons of this field, had to use rather picturesque language in their attempts to describe what kinds of forces love and its opposite really are. Ballou referred to "phrenomagnetic fluid" (or "vibes," in the lingo of our day). Emerson, slightly after him, said, people "imagine that they communicate their virtue and vice only by overt actions, and do not see that virtue and vice emit a breath every moment." In a sermon given in 1906 in Europe, Rabbi Aaron Tamaret used the most picturesque language of all:

> Good actions set good waves moving in the air, and a man performing good acts soon purifies the air which surrounds him. Evil actions poison the atmosphere, and a man's evil acts pollute the air until finally he himself breathes the poisonous vapors.... Were the eye able to perceive it, we should see that when a man raises his fist against another man, the air surrounding him is filled with waving fists; that when a man raises a foot to kick another man, the air registers feet raised high and aimed at him.

These writers were groping for images to describe an unseen force that is working in human affairs the way gravity or electricity is silently working in the world of matter. Nonviolence, as Kropotkin pointed out, is working to keep societies from falling apart as surely as electricity is holding proton and electron together in the atomic nucleus and gravity is keeping you and me from flying off the surface of the planet. In fact, we could call love for all, or nonviolence, a spiritual force of gravity. Though the attraction may seem weak at times, though it may even turn inside out and become repulsion, there is a force in the heart of every sentient creature that draws all life together spiritually. Gandhi did not invent but only discovered this force, in just the way that Sir Isaac Newton discovered the law of gravity. Both these pioneers made their epochal discoveries not by looking beyond the bounds of ordinary experience but by looking at ordinary experience in a new way. Hundreds of men and women had been hit by falling apples; millions have been subjected to indignities like being ejected from a railroad carriage. An occasional genius can use such common experiences to discover a law of gravity—or a law of love.

Long before Newton, men were using contrivances based on gravity. Long before Ballou or Tamaret or Gandhi, people were spontaneously being kind; people sought to mediate their differences, or nonviolently resist oppression, or rule justly in a hundred ways, many of them ingrained habits of behavior that perhaps date from prehuman existence. But a Newton or a Gandhi enables us to grasp the nature of this unseen force. Their experiments encourage us to surge ahead in the ways we use it. Gilbert, Maxwell, Edison, and many others made it possible for the same human beings who were clunking along with steam engines and communicating by carrier pigeon to spring forward into the modern age of power and electronics; in the same way—if enough of us pursue the discoveries of Thoreau or Gandhi or Martin Luther King—we can usher in a new age, in which, for example, neither individuals nor communities settle their differences by force but through cooperation.

There are, however, two salient differences between love for all and the other great natural forces like gravity and electricity. Whatever the latter actually are by nature—and science is far from being able to understand this—their laws can be determined with relative ease because they act primarily on matter. Nonviolence is different. Here an insight of Thoreau's can give us a valuable clue. Jailed for his refusal to pay taxes to a government that would use his money to support slavery and militarism, he pondered over his discovery of "civil disobedience":

> Again, I sometimes say to myself, when many millions of men ... demand of you a few shillings only, with the possibility, such is their constitution, of retracting or altering the present demand, . . . why expose yourself to this overwhelming brute force? You do not resist cold and hunger, the winds and the waves, thus obstinately; you quietly submit to a thousand similar necessities. . . . But just in proportion as I regard this as *not wholly a brute force, but partly a human force*, and consider that I have relations to those millions as to so many millions of men, and not of mere brute or inanimate things, I see that this appeal is possible, first and instantaneously, from them to the Maker of them, and secondly, from them to themselves.

In other words, Thoreau was saying that the force he was up against was not iron bars, nor even a faceless, impersonal "system." It was the will, the understanding in human beings like himself; and with human beings it is possible to communicate, either directly or by means of the unity that binds us all together, held by Thoreau to be our common "Maker." The power of nonviolence acts not on matter but on consciousness. And consciousness, of course, is what counts. Iron bars do not fly into position by themselves and entrap nonconformists, uranium does not mine itself; there is no violence in inanimate matter—and no capacity to respond to love.

The power of love for all may be more difficult to master than those of gravity and electricity, requiring of us an even deeper kind of commitment, and bringing into play a different level of human capability. On the other hand—and this is the second difference from physical forces—love for all cannot be mastered only to be misused. Gravity can be used to drop a bomb or electricity to kill, not to mention what nuclear energy can be used for. But, as a Christian mystic put it, "Love hath no errors, for all errors arise from the want of love." To become more loving is to become more wise and less injurious. I am not denying that handfuls of people are sometimes injured in nonviolent demonstrations, which, as all human activities, can be less than perfect. But can we compare this to the destruction of a nuclear holocaust or to the loss of millions each year to starvation and oppression?

THE SALT SATYĀGRAHA

Early in his career Gandhi rejected the term "passive resistance" for his experiments with putting love into practical, social action and coined the word *satyāgraha*. *Satyāgraha* means literally "holding fast to truth," but for Gandhi the word meant "soul force." Anyone who mastered this force found it more reliable and in the long run more effective than the familiar power that "grows out of the barrel of a gun," which is generally the weapon of choice in socialist and capitalist societies alike. Louis Fischer deserves the credit for recognizing that its well-timed application turned the tide of modern history. This occurred at the climax of the great Salt Satyāgraha in the struggle for India's independence.

The year was 1930. India was groaning under oppression and tense with revolutionary passion, but the people did not dare strike out violently—not only because they feared British retaliation but because everyone knew that at the first sign of violence Gandhi would call off the struggle as he had in 1922. What was their next move? Suddenly inspired, Gandhi informed the viceroy of the British *raj* that he was going to initiate civil disobedience against the salt law. One of the mechanisms of the British regime, common to economic exploitation everywhere, had been to step between the Indian citizenry and a vital necessity of life, by making it illegal for anyone to manufacture salt in that tropical country except government-supported monopolies. The prohibition imposed a very real hardship on the people, and the salt situation was a symbol of everything the British *raj* stood for in India.

Tension mounted as March 2, the appointed day, drew closer. On that morning Gandhi got up as usual, said his prayers, and with a group of seventy-eight chosen men and women from his spiritual community (they had published their names ahead of time in *Young India* for the convenience of the police) set out on foot for Dandi, a coastal village 200 miles to the south.

When they arrived twenty-four days later, their numbers grown to tens of thousands, Gandhi waded into the sea and, with every eye fixed on him, broke the salt law. He simply picked up a pinch of salt from the beach and in effect gave this message to India: "The salt law does not exist. We are free: Act accordingly."

He also informed the viceroy that, "God willing," he and his followers were going to help themselves to salt from the Dharasana salt pans, where "legal" manufactures were carried on. Long before the raid was to take place Gandhi was arrested, along with many others, by some estimates, 100,000. The mood of the police was ugly. On the day set for the raid, a nonviolent army of 2,500 volunteers led by Mrs. Sarojini Naidu, the poet, and Gandhi's second son, Manilal, hove into view on the road 150 miles north of Bombay that led into the Dharasana pans. Between them and the salt pans lay barbed wire, ditches filled with muddy water, and a force of 400 native police under the leadership of 6 British officers.

The police ordered the volunteers to stop. But at a signal the first-picked column of about 25 advanced from the group and proceeded slowly and in complete silence toward the pans. Now Fischer quotes from the grim eyewitness account of the American correspondent, Webb Miller:

> Suddenly at a word of command, scores of native policemen rushed upon the advancing marchers and rained blows on their heads with their steel-shod lathis [heavy batons]. Not one of the marchers even raised an arm to fend off the blows. They went down like ten-pins. From where I stood I heard the sickening whack of the clubs on unprotected skulls. The waiting crowd of marchers groaned and sucked in their breath in sympathetic pain at every blow. Those struck down fell sprawling, unconscious or writhing with fractured skulls or broken shoulders. . . .

The survivors, without breaking ranks, silently and doggedly marched on until struck down.

When all 25 were down, another column of 25 advanced slowly into certain injury and possible death, then another. By the time activities were halted because of the intense afternoon heat 320 were injured and 2 were killed. And India was free.

The Gandhi volunteers did not "take" the salt pans, either on that day or in the several days following, when the same grim scenes were repeated. The salt law was not yet repealed, and on paper India was still a colony. But after this display of determination, the world knew that it was only a matter of time before India would refuse to be ruled—and, as Fischer points out, England would refuse to rule. Rabindranath Tagore explained that "for Europe this is, in actual fact, a great moral defeat that has happened," but I prefer Fischer's viewpoint: "The British beat the Indians with batons and rifle butts. The Indians neither cringed nor complained nor retreated. That made England powerless and India invincible."

The nonviolent man or woman does not like suffering any more than you or I do. (Nonviolence toward all includes nonviolence toward oneself.) He or she knows, however, that we all have to face suffering sometimes rather than lie down under an injustice *or* inflict suffering on whoever is causing it. And when we choose to suffer this way we make the most direct appeal to the conscience of the other party—the "human force" in us speaks directly to the "human force" we are confronting.

Ideally, satyāgraha, as active love for all, is totally noninjurious. When we adopt it—when we "offer satyāgraha," as Gandhi would say—we try to save the exploiter as much as the exploited. However hard we try to turn others from what we perceive to be a wrong position, our purpose is not to leave them worse off in any way. One of the side effects of deterrence, as we saw, is it makes the other party more irrational. Satyāgraha makes them more rational. By appealing to conscience, it arouses conscience, making the other party that much more sensitive to the needs of others. For this reason deterrence contains the seeds of its own undoing, but satyāgraha contains seeds that are bound to bear fruit in the long run. By adopting it we may not get what we feel we want right away, and possibly not at all. We may not "win" in the terms we are usually tempted to apply. But whether or not we liberate our salt pans or get the government to send surplus food to China or induce our friend to give up a harmful habit, the nature of our appeal has helped those others a little. Future confrontations may well be less confrontational, and the final outcome is bound to be improvement.

Let's look at this from a government's point of view. Contrary to the usual notion we have of it, nonviolence can be used as well or better by a government than by the governed. Almost every government in the world constantly makes decisions about reliance on military force. Our government, like many others, faces a divided constituency on such issues. Setting aside the relative size of the dovish and hawkish factions for a moment, suppose a government simply wanted to do what was best, what would be most helpful in the long run, without regard to its immediate popularity. Such a government would be free to contemplate, say, a bold disarmament initiative. It would have no problem with the dove faction, of course; traditionally a small minority, the doves would be delighted. The other faction might well scream—for a while—and register its dissatisfaction by withdrawing support. But the government will have *taught* this faction something. It will have said, "In our judgment, we can safely pursue more peaceful methods of accommodation or persuasion in such conflicts." It will not have acted against interests of the hawk faction but against its fears and poor judgments, thus making its own job of governing easier in the long run. Not to do this—not to risk short-term unpopularity by educating the public to its own best interests—condemns a government to a perpetual round of crisis management and deepening ineptitude.

Take as another example the decisions states have to make about criminal justice. Some years back a British county adapted a technique used in the Netherlands and West Germany, permitting mild offenders to work off their offenses instead of going to prison. Why not have them do something useful for themselves and society instead of just "doing time"—and costing taxpayers money? It proved so successful that fifty-six other British counties adopted it the following year. And it succeeded because of its educational value. The county held the offenders responsible but did not condemn them. It said to the public, "These people are still part of our community; they are not 'criminals'; they have made a mistake, and they can make it good." As we saw in the last chapter, meaningful work gives people a sense of purpose and value and helps to decriminalize them. By this technique the offenders gained *and* society gained, an effective application of home-team strategies—and pure satyāgraha. In this country, where several states have adopted the same judicial reform and judges have discretionary powers to do so in juvenile cases, an Atlanta judge recently directed four youths who had gotten drunk and burned down a black church to help the parishioners rebuild it. This way the young men might even get to know the people they had offended, and thus make a small but long-term contribution to the whole racial situation. The alternative was sending them to prison, which would only encourage criminal self-images (and provide the requisite techniques).

Nonviolence, then, seeks lasting gains, not a rapid "win"; it always wants improved relations with the opposing party, never its submission. It operates by persuasion, not coercion. Shortly after William Penn was attracted to George Fox's way of life he asked Fox if he had to stop wearing a sword. Fox's answer was something like, "Wear thy sword as long as thou canst." He wanted Penn to outgrow the *need* for a sword and renounce it of his own free will. In the same way Gandhi never urged people to leave military service just to gratify him or anyone else; rather, he suggested they think the problem through and come to their own conclusions. "Error" was less to be shunned than insincerity. Fox and Gandhi strove constantly to move people's hearts but not to move them against their will. They wanted to educate their will, to free it from the compulsions of anger and fear, to help them get in touch with a deeper and wiser will inside themselves. Love, like gravity, works by bending the space around it so that the other's will moves into that new space. One is naturally and steadily drawn into the new position rather than shoved into it from behind. Although selfless love seems to operate slowly, it operates irresistibly, and what it gains is permanent.

Not all self-imposed suffering can create a curvature of spiritual space. If you were in Berkeley about twenty years ago, you might have seen a young man who planted himself on the sidewalk in front of KPFA, the listener-supported, liberal radio station, for several days. A sign around his neck explained that he was fasting against the station for not giving him a vote on their board of directors. The station was unimpressed. Before long the young man gave up and was seen making a beeline for the nearest coffee shop. It is not the mere technique of suffering that nonviolently persuades but the inner state of love.

We must consider one more important reason nonviolence is effective, before passing on to the biggest question before us, how to learn it. The American Gandhi scholar, Joan Bondurant, opens her landmark study by saying, "The technique to which Gandhi gave the name Satyāgraha is at once a mode of action and a method of enquiry." Within the small self-governing bodies like Quaker meetings or the old town halls that lie at the beginning of our political heritage, consensus, rather than voting, was the usual style. The idea was to distribute responsibility more evenly and prevent the political process from polarizing into a win-lose game that divides the community. It was also, and just as importantly, to ensure that the political process was not just a decision-making but a learning process for all concerned. "Through nonviolence," said Martin Luther King, "we avoid the temptation of taking on the psychology of victors." We also avoid the temptation of taking on the psychology of know-it-alls, or holier-than-thous. Quite apart from the salutary effect that this avoidance has on the other party, it is a great strategic advantage to ourselves, for it means that we are never "stumped." If the other party isn't budging an inch, we can continue to work at improving our own party, be it ourselves, an organization, or a movement. Gandhi often dropped back to work on Indian society when the British were unresponsive, and he usually made headway from the improved position—closer Hindu-Moslem unity, better training among the volunteers—on the next occasion.

One of the greatest nonviolent breakthroughs ever recorded on this continent, a kind of American Maritzburg, was accomplished by a revolutionary socialist named Ammon Hennacy while in solitary confinement in Atlanta Prison for refusing to serve in the "capitalist war" of 1917. In those days of war fever conscientious objectors were not in high esteem. Hennacy was not allowed to receive mail from his fiancée, his mother, or anyone else; his only human contact consisted in listening to guards maltreating a prisoner in a neighboring cell and in occasional visits from the warden, who wanted him to turn in his friends. Outside of a cot, a needle, and some thread, the only object in his cell was a Bible. But as he, perforce, read and reread the Bible, it started to make sense to him:

> Gradually I came to gain a glimpse of what Jesus meant when he said, "The Kingdom of God is within you." In my heart now after six months I could love everybody in the world but the warden, but if I did not love him then the Sermon on the Mount meant nothing at all. I really saw this

and felt it in my heart but I was too stubborn to admit it in my mind. One day I was walking back and forth in my cell when, in turning, my head hit the wall. Then the thought came to me: "Here I am locked up in a cell. The warden was never locked up in any cell and he never had a chance to know what Jesus meant. Neither did I until yesterday. So I must not blame him. I must love him." Now the whole thing was clear. This Kingdom of God must be in everyone: in the deputy, the warden, in the rat and the pervert—and now I came to know it—in myself . . . . *I would never have a better opportunity than this* to try out the Sermon on the Mount right now in my cell.

An "opportunity," that is, to "teach them another method: that of good will overcoming their evil intentions, or rather habits." This deep change of conviction in Hennacy caused the uncomprehending warden to offer him his release if he would spy for the Secret Service—and to let him go shortly after, even though he of course refused. And for Hennacy himself, the change was permanent. There are Ammon Hennacy houses today in several states that carry on his peacemaking ideals. What is so impressive in the Hennacy story is his almost total lack of external resources at that time: no typewriter, no publicity, no "support network," no library, no help from outside. But sometimes it takes a lack of external resources to make us turn to unsuspected resources from within; and that is where nonviolence comes from.

UPSTREAM TO UNITY

We now come to that most difficult question, the question toward which everything in this book has pointed: How do we change ourselves so that we can draw on these inner resources more effectively? Lacking this element of inner cultivation, 90 percent of what people call nonviolence today is really only an attempt to influence others without going as far as physical violence. The positive element of love for the other party is conspicuous by its absence, while the absence of the violent element is sometimes temporary. Most of us who are for good reasons opposed to war keep finding ourselves opposed to people who represent war, even though we feel we should keep the two distinct. In the same way, governmental efforts at arbitration are justified because they "save money"; the Camp David peace attempt was made because the United States needed to stabilize relations in the Middle East, not out of selfless love of peace.

This is not to deprecate such efforts; it is only to say that we cannot hope to understand or evaluate nonviolence through them. The degree of commitment—*personal* commitment—behind them is very small. People try this "nonviolence" for about a week, as Theodore Roszak somewhere points out, decide it doesn't "work," and go back to the same methods that have failed to work for centuries.

But Gandhi felt that nonviolence was infallible. After fifty years' experience he was convinced that every apparent failure of nonviolence stemmed from shortcomings in the person or persons trying to use that force, not in the force itself. Gravity is not running down; there is never less electrical potential in the universe. But the instruments we fallible mortals build to use these forces inevitably have problems with friction and resistance.

Yet "there comes a time," said Gandhi, "when the individual becomes irresistible and his action is all-pervasive in its effect. That comes when he reduces himself to zero"; that is, when he or she presents *no* more internal resistance to the force of love. And how is this transformation to come about? One obviously necessary change, as we have seen, is reversing the priorities in our values. An American GI, undergoing strenuous training for Vietnam, wrote in his diary, "They work us harder than the average college student. But there's a reason. We are learning to kill, while the college student is learning how to live." The priority has got to be quite reversed; a society (like an organism) has to choose life, actively and completely, if it wants to live. We have also seen how in a subtler way me-ism does nothing but increase the distance between what we perceive to be our personal satisfaction and the welfare of all, causing friction within us because it is only in the latter sphere that our own real welfare can be realized. This process only increases our internal resistance to the force of love for all. The socially reinforced value put on separateness, or what a colleague of mine, Robert Bellah, calls "secular individualism," has also to be turned inside out.

But, in the last analysis, a value transformation must be won by the internal struggle that goes on in every one of us, almost regardless of where society is going or what it does. "Upon the whole," said Erasmus centuries ago, "the first and most important step towards peace is earnestly to desire it." In 1934, the British essayist Storm Jameson wrote prophetically that while we all *wish* for peace, unfortunately we do not *will* it, and about the same time George Orwell wrote, in *The Road to Wigan Pier*, that "economic injustice will stop the moment we want it to stop . . . and if we genuinely want it to stop the method adopted hardly matters."

Desires are the raw material of love. If the same desires we now feel for little pleasures, for a better job, for a new tie, for a piece of cake, for more prestige—all things that will disappear in half an hour if a major war breaks out—were gathered up into one great desire for peace, our inner resistance to the force of love for all would disappear.

It is sometimes overlooked, behind the glamour of Gandhi's personality and the drama of the Indian situation, that fifteen or twenty years of dogged, almost military self-discipline lay behind the conversion of ordinary Indian women and men into an irresistible flood of love that broke down the barriers of imperialism. One of these men was future prime minister Jawaharlal Nehru. Here is how he describes his inner struggle when mounted police charged a peaceful demonstration he had been in two years earlier in Lucknow:

> All I knew was that I had to stay where I was and must not yield or go back. I felt half blinded with the blows, and sometimes a dull anger seized me and a desire to hit out. I thought how easy it would be to pull down the police officer in front of me from his horse and to mount up myself, but *long training and discipline held*, and I did not raise a hand, except to protect my face from a blow.

How much the people in India must have wanted independence to so transform themselves that if need be they could up to a point master their instinctive impulse to fight or flee. How many things they must have done without, committing themselves to decades of struggle until they convinced themselves and the British that they would not stop until they achieved that goal.

Can we make do with less? Can those of us who have seen the grave dangers in the mounting tide of violence hope to prevail against it with less commitment of inner strength? As far as the basic human material is concerned, we face the same challenge today that Nehru and thousands of nameless satyāgraha volunteers in India faced and overcame.

In outer respects, however, our situation is a little different. We have neither a Gandhi to inspire us nor an obvious foreign invader to work against. All the more reason, then, to work on our inner lives. We need a way to grapple with our desires; to concentrate them, redirect them, harmonize them with our conscience and better judgment, even if the effort takes a lifetime. That way is meditation.

It would require another volume to extricate this word from the confusion that usually settles around it. But let me say that by "meditation" I do not refer to letting the mind wander, free associating, relaxing, or thinking something over. Meditation is a disciplined, determined effort to bring the mind under control. It requires skilled guidance and almost unbelievable personal dedication. It makes us progressively less likely to respond with anger, for example, just because we have met with anger, progressively freer to respond however a situation requires, and progressively more able to keep on working at an unsatisfactory situation until it improves. Meditation is the most powerful of all tools for increasing our sensitivity to injustice, and at the same time for learning to transform our anger into a constructive force in the way that we discussed in Chapter 6 of this book.

Meditation is a universal human capacity. It has sustained great visionaries and activists throughout the Western tradition as well as in India and the East. Like nonviolence, it has roots even in America. Lewis Mumford is one of the commentators on our times who has seen this. For Mumford, violence and pornography, far from being as native as apple pie, are direct threats to our American heritage. He says when speaking of Emerson's mother, who used to practice something like meditation an hour every day, "This is an essential beginning: that we should slow down our activities. There's nothing so pressing that you have to desert your inner self."

The mad rush for money, for prestige, and —ironically—the search for "me," is precisely that: a desertion of our inner selves. Slowing down gives us more time to become more aware of who we are—and simultaneously more aware of others. The inner self is where we make the most gratifying discovery of our relationship with the whole.

It is also from this deepest self that we draw the resources with which to make serious, permanent, and intentional changes in our own lives. This is individual economics. Just as we need external sources of physical energy for the kind of employment that builds up the gross national product, we need spiritual energy for full spiritual employment as responsible human beings. The source of spiritual energy is within us, and meditation is simply a way—the supreme way, as far as my knowledge goes—of drilling for it. That is why to make the fullest contribution of which we are capable, meditation, which is not a substitute for work but a way to fuel and to orient our work, is indispensable.

All of us need rootedness in our inner selves, and this need gets ever stronger as the drift toward violence and disunity cuts us off from that dimension of our being. Our culture's lack of a recent tradition of meditation and related disciplines (and meditation, again, is nothing if not a discipline) is therefore critical. Reliable experience and information about how to deepen our interior lives has become, though we don't quite realize it, one of the most vital resources of our time.

I believe that when people like Fox and King and Gandhi said that the source of their strength was prayer, what I am calling meditation is essentially what they meant. Meditation is not a "substitute for religion," as some have charged, but there is a connection. For meditation, and the work that flows from it, is our surest escape from "secular individualism." We need access to some source of inexhaustible security to get our bearings in this confusing world and to face the storms we will certainly sail into when we decide to go against the conditioning of our times. And "call it by whatever name you like," said Gandhi, "that which gives one the greatest solace in the midst of the severest fire is God."

EPILOGUE

Seven years ago I brought home the first copy of my book on the poems of Homer. My children were tickled to see their father's name on the cover but could not relate to anything on its footnoted pages. They said, "Now write a children's book, Daddy." I have always felt there was some justice in the appeal, and it bothered me that they would be practically old enough to write books of their own by the time *America Without Violence* was finished.

But I feel, Jess and Josh, that this *is* a children's book, perhaps the kind you wanted most. Just recently, as you know, a nephew was born into our family, a ray of joy for us all. I understand his parents planted a peach tree in front of their house the day he was born. They are well-read people and must have known that they were following an age-old practice, but the conscious knowledge hardly seems to have diminished the force of the ancient symbol. Surely the most cherished hope of parents always is that their children grow up straight and vigorous and long-lived as a tree. And shall that hope be vain?

Glancing over at the magazine the man beside me on the bus is reading, I see an ad for saving the whales on one page and an ad for cheap handguns on the other. We are coming north out of Richmond and have just passed between two billboards, a sexy ad for cigarettes pitched especially at young people and a low-budget, public service message on the dangers of cancer. Today the choice between life and death confronts us at every turn. It is the choice of our age, and we cannot escape it. Even to think that we have no choice is to have made the wrong one. That has been the message of this book.

REFERENCES AND NOTES

What follows are sources for direct quotations and most other "hard" facts cited in the text, listed by book page number. Also included are a few comments and indications of sources of additional information. All italics in the text are mine unless otherwise indicated.

PREFACE

x Humanities colleague: René Girard, *Violence and the Sacred* (Baltimore: Johns Hopkins, 1977) 33.
Psychiatrist: Samuel Yochelson, in *The National Observer*, July 11, 1977. I am otherwise in strong sympathy with both Professor Girard and Dr. Yochelson.

1 / THE LIE OF OTHERNESS

3 *Living with Terrorism:* R. L. Clutterbuck, *New Yorker*, June 12, 1978.
Increase of terrorism: cf. Paul Wehr, *Conflict Regulation* (Boulder: Westview Press, 1979) 104, 106.
Knud Larsen: *Aggression: Myths and Models* (Chicago: University of Chicago Press, 1976) 287.
4 116 percent increase: L. Kupperstein and W. C. Wilson, "Erotica and Anti-social Behavior," *Technical Report of the Commission on Obscenity and Pornography* (Washington, D.C.: U.S. Government Printing Office, 1970) 311–24.
B. F. Skinner, *Beyond Freedom and Dignity* (New York: Knopf, 1971) 3.
5 Accidental shootings: J. Chris Gillin, M.D., and Frank W. Ochberg, M.D. "Firearms Control and Violence," *The Stanford MD* 8:2 (Spring 1969) 22. For more recent (and much higher) figures, see Irvin Block, *Gun Control: One Way to Save Lives: Public Affairs Pamphlet No. 536* (New York: Public Affairs Committee, 1976) 11.
Guns and Ammo for April 1975; cited in fund-raising letter of the National Coalition to Ban Handguns, n.d.
Five times as likely: Matthew G. Yeager, *How Well Does the Handgun Protect You and Your Family?* (Washington, D.C.: U.S. Conference of Mayors, 1976) 11. See also its *Handgun Control: Issues and Alternatives*, pp. 7–8.
Twice as likely: from a National Coalition to Ban Handguns letter.

6 Detroit, 1967: Franklin E. Zimring and George D. Newton, Jr., *Firearms and Violence in American Life, A Staff Report to the National Commission on the Causes and Prevention of Violence* (Washington, D.C.: U.S. Government Printing Office, 1970) 64; also Dorothy T. Samuel, *Safe Passage on City Streets* (Nashville: Abingdon, 1975; available from the Fellowship of Reconciliation, Nyack, N.Y.) 56.

Rural Ohio study: *Christian Science Monitor,* February 25, 1977. See also *How Well Does the Handgun Protect You?,* p. 5.

Stolen handguns: *How Well Does the Handgun Protect You?,* p. 7.

7 Two-thirds not premeditated: Sometimes this figure is closer to three-fourths; cf. Block, *Gun Control,* p. 14.

Victim precipitation: Donald Lunde, *Murder and Madness* (Stanford, Calif.: Stanford, 1975) 9. Displaying a weapon leads to injuries among robbery victims that are five times more serious; see also *How Well Does the Handgun Protect You?,* p. 2.

Experienced felon: Ann Landers column in the *San Francisco Examiner & Chronicle,* June 24, 1979.

Quaker who lost his nerve: One version of this story is in Adin Ballou, *Christian Non-Resistance in all its Important Bearings, Illustrated and Defended* (Philadelphia: J. M. M'Kim, 1846; now available in facsimile reprint: Englewood, N.J.: Jerome S. Ozer, 1972) 163, 167; for another, see Margaret E. Hirst, "The Stand for Peace," in *George Fox: Some Modern Appreciations* (London: Swarthmore Press, 1925) 114.

8 Lunde: *Murder and Madness,* p. 9.

W. J. Bowers and G. L. Pierce: "Deterrence or Brutalization: What Is the Effect of Executions?" *Crime and Delinquency* 26:4 (Oct. 1980) 453–84. Similarly, there is evidence to suggest that "security" devices in stores encourage shoplifting.

9 S. E. Samenow and S. Yochelson: *The National Observer,* July 11, 1977.

Robert C. Johansen, *Jimmy Carter's National Security Policy: A World-Order Critique. World Order Models Project Working Paper No. 14* (New York: Institute for World Order, 1980) 29.

10 Einstein: Norman Cousins, *Human Options* (New York: Norton, 1981) 24.

11 Einstein letter: *New York Times,* March 29, 1972.

12 Lunde: *Murder and Madness,* p. 71.

12–13 Kenneth E. Boulding, *Stable Peace* (Austin: University of Texas Press, 1978) 80.

13 Robert Jay Lifton, *Home from the War* (New York: Simon & Schuster, 1973) 126, describing the alienation of veterans returning from Vietnam.

13–14 1980 crime figures: from the annual FBI report; quotations from the *San Francisco Chronicle,* October 23, 1980.

15 The shah and Somoza: *Christian Science Monitor,* April 10, 1979.

2 / THE USES OF VIOLENCE

18 Boulevard Nights and *The Warriors*: *Christian Science Monitor,* April 4, 1979.

19 FDR and Richard Nixon: Robert Jewett and John S. Lawrence, *The American Monomyth* (Garden City, N.Y.: Anchor Books, 1977) 38–39, 138–39.

Nicholas Johnson: testimony before PTA television violence hearings, February 1977.

19–20 Statistics: as compiled by Dr. Anne Somers in her excellent article, "Violence, Television, and the Health of American Youth," *New England Journal of Medicine* 294:15 (Apr. 8, 1976) 811–17; supplemented from Alberta E. Siegel, "Televised Violence: Recent Research on Its Effects," in *Aggression* (Research Publication 52, Association for Research in Nervous and Mental Disease, 1974) 271–83, and the surgeon general's report, *Television and Growing Up: The Impact of Televised Violence* (Washington, D.C.: U.S. Government Printing Office, 1972).

20 "Effect" statistics: from Lunde, *Murder and Madness,* and the *Sourcebook on Criminal Justice Statistics* (Albany, N.Y.: U.S. Department of Justice, Criminal Justice Research Center, 1979).

Berkeley High: the *Daily Californian,* March 12, 1979.

21 Helter-Skelter: Jewett and Lawrence, *American Monomyth,* pp. 38, 209. For other examples, see Terry Orlick, *Winning Through Cooperation* (Washington, D.C.: Acropolis, 1978) 81.

22 Belson study: Howard Muson, "Teenage Violence and the Telly," *Psychology Today* 12:2 (Mar. 1978) 50–54. See now William Belson's *Television Violence and the Adolescent Boy* (Lexington, Mass.: Lexington, 1978).

EEG specialist: Jerry Mander, *Four Arguments in Favor of the Elimination of Television* (New York: Morrow, 1978) 211.

23 "Large-scale dolls": *Christian Science Monitor,* April 4, 1979.

24 Susan Atkins: Orlick, *Winning Through Cooperation,* p. 79.

San Francisco psychiatrist: Dr. James C. Bozzuto, quoted in the *San Francisco Examiner,* December 14, 1976.

26 "Television enters powerfully": *To Establish Justice, to Insure Domestic Tranquility: Final Report of the National Commission on the Causes and Prevention of Violence* (Washington, D.C.: U.S. Government Printing Office, 1969) 195.

New Jersey experiment: *Wall Street Journal,* January 6, 1982.

27 The Warriors: Christian Science Monitor, April 4, 1979.

27–28 Assassin: San Francisco Chronicle, April 28, 1977.

28 Dr. Franz Inglefinger, *New England Journal of Medicine* 294:15 (Apr. 8, 1976) 838.

Walter Lippman: quoted in A. M. Schlesinger, Jr., *Violence: America in the Sixties* (New York: New American Library, 1968) 60–61.

3 / PUBLIC ENEMY NUMBER ONE

31 Confucius: quoted by Huston Smith, *Forgotten Truth* (New York: Harper & Row, 1976) 150.

32–33 The Mbuti: Colin M. Turnbull, "The Politics of Non-Aggression (Zaire)," in Ashley Montagu, ed., *Learning Non-Aggression* (New York: Oxford University Press, 1978) 161–221. My direct quotes are respectively from pp. 175 and 199.

33 Wendell Berry, *The Unsettling of America: Culture and Agriculture* (San Francisco: Sierra Club, 1977).

34 Schweitzer: quoted in *Fellowship* 45:1–2 (Jan.–Feb. 1979) 23.

Pediatrician: Richard J. Feinbloom, M.D., "TV Update," *Pediatrics* 62:3 (Sept. 1978) 430.

35 M. Klaus, M.D., and J. H. Kennell, M.D., *Maternal-Infant Bonding* (St. Louis: Mosby, 1976) 1–2.

Reunited families: Marie Winn, *The Plug-In Drug: Television, Children, and the Family* (New York: Viking, 1977) 214; *Wall Street Journal,* January 6, 1982.

36 Foundlings: James J. Lynch, *The Broken Heart: The Medical Consequences of Loneliness* (New York: Basic Books, 1977) 76–77.

Roseto: ibid., 16–25.

37 Dan White: *Christian Science Monitor,* December 1, 1978.

38 Figure 1: from Lunde, *Murder and Madness,* p. 2.

39 Figure 2: adapted from *Homicide in the United States: 1900–1964* (Washington, D.C.: National Center for Health Statistics, n.d.); extended with data from annual FBI *Uniform Crime Reports.*

Schweitzer: conversations with Norman Cousins; see Cousins's *Human Options* (New York: Norton, 1981) 23.

40 Brooklyn psychiatrist: Dr. Denise Shine, quoted in Winn, *Plug-In Drug,* p. 74.

James Baldwin, "Fifth Avenue Uptown," reprinted in William Smart, *Eight Modern Essayists* (New York: St. Martin's, 1973) 337.

Haldane: quoted in R. B. Lal, *The Gita in the Light of Modern Science* (Bombay: Somaiya, 1970) 25.

Mother Teresa: Committee Chairman John Sanness quoted by *San Francisco Examiner,* December 10, 1979; ecstatic Bengali in *San Francisco Chronicle,* same date.

41 D. W. Johnson: Orlick, *Winning Through Cooperation,* p. 105.

Baldwin: "Fifth Avenue Uptown," p. 343.

42 Nuremberg project: Urie Bronfenbrenner, "The Origins of Alienation," *Scientific American* 231 (Aug. 1974) 61. See also Arthur Kornhaber, M.D., and Kenneth L. Woodward, *Grandparents/Grandchildren: The Vital Connection* (New York: Doubleday, 1981).

André Trocmé: Philip Hallie, *Lest Innocent Blood Be Shed* (New York: Harper & Row, 1979). Highly recommended.

Raoul Wallenberg: See, for example, the *Christian Science Monitor* for July 23, 1980.

43 Ballou, *Christian Non-Resistance,* p. 10.

44 Peter Kropotkin, *Mutual Aid: A Factor in Evolution* (Boston: Porter Sargent, Extending Horizons, 1980; original ed., 1902) 276.

Auto deaths: *U.S. News & World Report,* July 14, 1980.

45 Dan White: *Christian Science Monitor,* December 1, 1978.

46 Fatal shootings: Lunde, *Murder and Madness,* p. 27.

Weinstein shooting: personal communication from neighbors.

47 Susan Atkins: Orlick, *Winning Through Cooperation,* p. 79.

4 / THE ANSWER OF EVOLUTION

51 Gandhi: Krishna Kripalani, ed., *All Men Are Brothers* (Ahmedabad: Navajivan, 1960) 110; p. 77 of the World Without War Publications edition (1972). The context is: "The first condition of non-violence is justice all round in every department of life. Perhaps, it is too much to expect of human nature. I do not, however, think so. No one . . ."

51–52 Plato: *Protagoras* 320C–323A. A similar story will be found in Hesiod's *Works and Days,* ll. 276–80.

53 Mammalian evolution: Guy Bush et al., "Rapid Speciation and Chromosomal Evolution in Mammals," *Proceedings of the National Academy of Sciences* 74 (1977) 3942.

54 Norman Cousins, *The Improbable Triumvirate* (New York: Norton, 1972) 152–53.

McKenna decision: cited by Chief Justice Warren, *Trop* v. *Dulles,* 356 U.S. 101 (October term, 1957).

55 Popularizer: Robert Ardrey, in *African Genesis;* quoted by Ashley Montagu, "Human Aggression," *The Sciences* 17:8 (Dec. 1977) 7.

Tarzan: from the original novel; quoted in an unpublished manuscript furnished the author by Erling Holtsmark.

57 Kropotkin: *Mutual Aid,* p. 5.

57-58 E. O. Wilson: quoted by Richard Salzmann, "The Future and Montessori," *N.A.M.T.A. Quarterly* 4:3 (Spring 1979) 37.

58 Stephen Jay Gould: "Sociobiology: The Art of Storytelling," *New Scientist,* November 16, 1978, p. 532.

"The idea": Ashley Montagu, *The Nature of Human Aggression* (New York: Oxford University Press, 1976) 67.

Leakey: Richard Leakey and Roger Lewin, *Origins: What New Discoveries Reveal about the Emergence of Our Species and Its Possible Future* (New York: Dutton, 1977) 211.

58-59 "Are we to believe": Anatol Rapaport, "Approaches to Theories of Large Scale Human Conflicts," in Hugh Freeman, ed., *Progress in Mental Health* (London: Churchill, 1969) 41.

59 Enervation of facial expression: conversations with Sherwood Washburn.

Stimulation of "centers": Montagu, *Nature of Human Aggression,* pp. 199-200.

60 Expert on terrorism: R. L. Clutterbuck; interview in *New Yorker,* June 12, 1978, p. 37.

"Blow up the next guy's plant": ibid., p. 61.

Erich Fromm, *The Anatomy of Human Destructiveness* (New York: Holt, 1973) 23 (his italics).

60-61 Mary Midgley, "Gene-Juggling," *Philosophy* 54:210 (Oct. 1979) 455 (her italics).

61 Auden: Anne Freemantle and W. H. Auden, *The Protestant Mystics* (Boston: Little, Brown, 1964) 3-4.

Tokyo: *The Times* (London), July 23, 1980, p. 8. Other comparisons: Montagu, "Human Aggression," p. 9.

62 Viktor Frankl, *Man's Search for Meaning,* rev. ed. (New York: Pocket Books, 1963) 168.

63 Biologist: Paul Campbell, quoted in Lal, *The Gita,* p. 29.

63-64 Peaceable societies: David Fabbro, "Peaceful Societies: An Introduction," *Journal of Peace Research* 15:1 (1978) 67-83; Montagu, *Learning Non-Aggression.*

64 The Koster dig: Stuart Struever and Felicia Antonelli Holton, *Koster: Americans in Search of Their Prehistoric Past* (Garden City, N.Y.: Anchor Books, 1979) 258.

65 Old Europeans: Marija Gimbutas, "The First Wave of Eurasian Steppe Pastoralists into Copper Age Europe," *Journal of Indo-European Studies* 5 (1977) 281.

The Tasaday: Montagu, *Nature of Human Aggression,* p. 167. For another view of the Tasaday and the other peaceful peoples cited, and a balanced account of their aggressiveness, see Irenäus Eibl-Eibesfeldt, *The Biology of Peace and War: Men, Animals, and Aggression* (New York: Viking, 1979), chaps. 6, 7.

66 Civilized Bushmen: Montagu, *Nature of Human Aggression,* p. 170.

Competitiveness in !Kung sports: Patricia Draper, quoted in ibid., p. 171. See also R. K. Dentan, *The Semai: A Nonviolent People of Malaya* (New York: Holt, 1968) 59.

67 The Maori: Andrew P. Vayda, "Maoris and Muskets in New Zealand: Disruption of a War System," *Political Science Quarterly* 85 (1970) 560–84. For further details see his *War in Ecological Perspective* (New York: Plenum, 1976) 75–102.

68 Lorenz data: *On Aggression* (New York: Harcourt, Brace & World, 1966) 129–30, 198–99; *Motivation of Human and Animal Behavior* (New York: Van Nostrand Reinhold, 1973) 106.

Fighting in animals: Michael W. Fox, "Man and Nature: Biological Perspectives," in R. K. Morris and M. W. Fox, eds., *On the Fifth Day* (Washington, D.C.: Acropolis, 1978) 114.

69 Tasaday evasion tactics: Peggy Durdin, "From the Space Age to the Tasaday Age," *New York Times Magazine,* October 8, 1971. This tactic also has been observed among the Mbuti (Fabbro, "Peaceful Societies," p. 72), the !Kung, and other groups.

John Spenkelink: *Time,* June 4, 1970.

5 / FORGOTTEN HISTORY

70 Wordsworth: *Tintern Abbey,* ll. 34–35.

Midgley: "Gene-Juggling," p. 444.

70–71 Brezhnev and Rao: *San Francisco Chronicle,* June 9, 1980.

71 M. Lavisse: Tolstoy, *Christianity and Patriotism* (London: Cape, 1922) 483.

R. Coudenhove-Kalergi, *From War to Peace* (London: Cape, 1959) 102; discussed in M. Melko, *52 Peaceful Societies* (Oakville, Ontario: Canadian Peace Research Institute, 1973) 8.

72 Gandhi, *Hind Swaraj* (Ahmedabad: Navajivan, 1938) 130.

73 Fox: John W. Graham, "George Fox," in *George Fox: Some Modern Appreciations,* p. 40.

74 Penn: quoted in Rufus Jones, ed., *The Journals of George Fox* (New York: Capricorn, 1963) 63.

Quaker peace testimony: ibid., p. 128. In a letter of 1659 Fox wrote: "All that pretend to fight for Christ are deceived; for His Kingdom is not of this world, therefore his servants do not fight . . ."; see *George Fox: Some Modern Appreciations*, p. 42.

Penn's letter: reprinted in Staughton Lynd, *Nonviolence in America: A Documentary History* (New York: Bobbs-Merrill, 1966) 4–5.

Penn's penal reforms: Stephen G. Cary et al., *Speak Truth to Power: A Quaker Search for an Alternative to Violence* (Philadelphia: American Friends Service Committee, 1955) 37. The quotation on "workhouses" is from the State Charter of Pennsylvania.

76 Judith M. Brown, "Makers of the Twentieth Century: Mohandas Karamchand Gandhi," *History Today* 30 (May 1980) 19.

Germantown Friends: Cary et al., *Speak Truth to Power*, p. 38.

76 John Woolman: "Considerations on Keeping Negroes," in Amelia Mott Gummere, ed., *The Journals and Essays of John Woolman* (New York: Macmillan, 1922) 338.

77 Trevelyan: quoted in *The Journal of John Woolman and a Plea for the Poor* (New York: Corinth, 1961) ix–x.

The Suffolk Resolves: Gene Sharp, "Disregarded History: The Power of Nonviolent Action," *Fellowship* 42:3 (March 1976) 8.

Ibid. This was felt to be the case much earlier by Charles K. Whipple, in 1839; see Robert Cooney and Helen Michalowski, *The Power of the People* (Culver City, Calif.: Peace Press, 1977) 26.

Jonathan Dymond, "The Probable Practical Effects of Adhering to the Moral Law in Respect to War," quoted in Ballou, *Christian Non-Resistance*, p. 177.

78 Ballou: *Christian Non-Resistance*, p. 235.

Galbraith: *The New Industrial State* (New York: Mentor, 1972) 142.

79 Arbitration developments: Charles Chatfield, *Peace Movements in America* (New York: Schocken, 1973).

Liberal internationalism: Sandi Cooper, "The Impact of Nationalism on European Peace Movements and Liberal Internationalists," *Peace and Change* 6:1/2 (1980) 23–36, and his bibliography.

Pacifism: See Peter Brock, *Pacifism in the United States* (Princeton, N.J.: Princeton, 1968).

80 Martin Luther King, *Stride Toward Freedom: The Montgomery Story* (New York: Harper & Row, 1964) 78–79.

Sayre: See John M. Swomley, "John Nevin Sayre: Part II," *Fellowship*

44:6 (June 1978) 6–9.

Page: Harold E. Fey, ed., *Kirby Page, Social Evangelist* (Nyack, N.Y.: Fellowship of Reconciliation, 1975) 90.

81 Szent-Györgyi: quoted in William Shirer, *Gandhi: A Memoir* (New York: Simon & Schuster, 1979) 12. A highly recommended book.

82 Norwegian schoolteachers' strike and Berlin: T. K. Mahadevan, Adam Roberts, and Gene Sharp, *Civilian Defense: An Introduction* (New Delhi: Gandhi Peace Foundation, 1967) 188–92. For other examples, see Hannah Arendt, *Eichmann in Jerusalem* (New York: Penguin, 1977) chap. 10, and Philip Hallie, *Lest Innocent Blood Be Shed.*

84 Burritt: quoted in Lynd, *Nonviolence in America*, p. 94.

Dellinger: in ibid., p. 521.

84–85 The "notable comparison": *Civilian Defense*, p. 210.

85–86 Czech uprising: Cary et al., *Speak Truth to Power*, p. 63 (their italics).

86 Leonard C. Lewin, *Report from Iron Mountain* (New York: Dial, 1967) 104–5, n. 9.

87 National peace academy: See now the report, *To Establish the United States Academy of Peace* (Washington, D.C.: U.S. Government Printing Office, 1981).

JROTC: reported in the *Reporter for Conscience' Sake* 36 (1979).

Boulding: *Stable Peace*, p. 69.

87–88 Patricia Mische, "Women, Power and Alternative Futures, Part II: Women and Power," *Whole Earth Papers* 1:9 (1979).

6 / THE HOME-TEAM STRATEGY

89 "Caught up in the game": *San Francisco Examiner & Chronicle*, October 24, 1976.

Captain Nevill's game: Paul Fussell, *The Great War and Modern Memory* (New York: Oxford University Press, 1979) 27.

Football war: Montagu, *Nature of Human Aggression*, p. 279.

90 "Right or wrong": Ralph Leef, in the *Santa Rosa Press-Democrat*, January 5, 1978.

"Terrific combination" and "good" vs. "bad" violence: *San Francisco Examiner & Chronicle*, October 24, 1976.

All-China chairman: Orlick, *Winning Through Cooperation*, p. 69.

!Kung sports: Draper, in Montagu, *Nature of Human Aggression*, p. 171; see also notes for p. 66.

91 Winn: *Plug-In Drug*, pp. 83–84.

William Bruns and Thomas Tutko, *Winning is Everything* (New York: Macmillan, 1976).

Tyranny of competition: Ian Jackson, in *San Francisco Examiner,* April 1, 1979.

92 John Kenneth Galbraith, *Annals of an Abiding Liberal* (Boston: Houghton Mifflin, 1979) 339.

President Johnson: Richard J. Barnet, *The Giants: Russia and America* (New York: Simon & Schuster, 1977) 24–25.

Elliot Aronson, *The Social Animal* (San Francisco: Freeman, 1976) 153–54.

93 Professor Raiffa: Gaither lecture at University of California at Berkeley, Fall 1980.

Colin M. Turnbull, *The Forest People: A Study of the Pygmies of the Congo* (New York: Touchstone, 1962) 118.

94 CRS clips: collected in its publication, *Examples of CRS Aid to Communities* (Sept. 1977); additional information courtesy of Julius Klugman, CRS regional director in San Francisco.

96 Reston: *San Francisco Chronicle & Examiner,* November 27, 1977.

Jehan Sadat: *Christian Science Monitor,* December 27, 1976.

97 Arbatov: Franklin Griffiths and John C. Polanyi, *The Dangers of Nuclear War,* Pugwash Conference No. 30 (Toronto: University of Toronto Press, 1979) 151.

98 Edmund Blunden, *The Mind's Eye* (NewYork: Arno, 1934) 38.

Gandhi at Maritzburg: *An Autobiography, or the Story of My Experiments with Truth* (Ahmedabad: Navajivan, 1948) 140–41.

99 Gandhi: R. K. Prabhu and U. R. Rao, *The Mind of Mahatma Gandhi,* rev. ed. (Ahmedabad: Navajivan, 1967) 16.

His anxious doctors: William Shirer, *Gandhi: A Memoir* (New York: Simon & Schuster, 1979) 188.

Ashadevi Aryanayakam: from the BBC documentary film *Gandhi's India.* Highly recommended.

Shirer: *Gandhi: A Memoir,* p. 28.

100 "Such a struggle": Krishna Kripalani, ed., *All Men Are Brothers,* reprint ed. (Chicago: World Without War, 1972) 78.

"My non-cooperation": Eknath Easwaran, *Gandhi the Man,* 2d ed. (Petaluma, Calif.: Nilgiri Press, 1978) 56.

7 / THE ACID TEST: WAR AND PEACE

106 First strike: See Robert C. Aldridge, *The Counterforce Syndrome, Transnational Institute Pamphlet No. 7,* n.d.

Russian reactions: *Christian Science Monitor,* March 31, 1980; Vasily Kuznetzov: *Washington Post,* October 1, 1979. For another sobering view of the missile crisis, see Garry Wills, "The Kennedy Imprisonment: 2. Prisoner of Toughness," *Atlantic Monthly,* February 1982.

107 General Brown: quoted in R. J. Rummell, *Peace Endangered: The Reality of Détente* (Beverly Hills, Calif.: Sage Publications, 1977) 57.

Professor York: from *Physics Today,* January 1977, quoted by John C. Hopkins, "Why Not Stop Testing?" *Bulletin of the Atomic Scientists* 33:4 (Apr. 1977) 32.

G. D. Deshingkar, "Deterrence: With Weapons or Without?" *Alternatives* 4:1 (1978) 140. See also Norman Cousins, *In Place of Folly* (New York: Washington Square, 1962) 103: "[Deterrence] invokes irrational force as the principal means of creating rational restraint."

108 Senator Vandenberg: Sidney Lens, "Thirty Years of Escalation," *The Nation,* May 27, 1978, p. 626.

Unemployment figures: Robert C. Johansen, *Towards a Dependable Peace* (New York: Institute for World Order, 1978) 53, n. 30. Senator McGovern reports that 30 percent of our military spending would create from 2 to 5 million more jobs in solar energy and public transportation (from a circular letter, n.d.).

Boulding: lectures delivered at University of California at Berkeley, February 1982.

109 Lloyd Dumas, "National Insecurity in the Nuclear Age," *Bulletin of the Atomic Scientists* 32:5 (May 1976) 34.

Admiral LaRocque: Jonathan Leonard, "Danger: Nuclear War," *Harvard Magazine* (Nov.–Dec. 1980) 23.

Barnet: *Giants,* p. 173.

110 *The Conqueror: San Francisco Examiner & Chronicle,* August 5, 1979. Dr. John Gofman (see next note) tells me that he has not been able to document this account scientifically.

John Gofman, M.D., "The Plutonium Controversy," *Journal of the American Medical Association* 236:3 (July 1976) 285. See now Dr. Gofman's definitive book, *Radiation and Human Health* (San Francisco: Sierra Club, 1981).

111 Saint Augustine: *Confessions,* I.18.

112 Ambassador Tsarapkin: *Arms Control Report: The U.S. Arms Control and Disarmament Agency* (Washington, D.C.: U.S. Government Printing Office, 1978) 10.

"No choice": *Christian Science Monitor,* May 19, 1977; John G. Hubbell in *Reader's Digest,* January 1979, p. 69.

Emerson: "War," in Arthur and Lila Weinberg, *Instead of Violence*

(Boston: Beacon Press, 1963) 378–79.

Barnet: *Giants,* p. 155.

113 Edgar Mitchell: from a brochure of Planetary Citizens, n.d.

114 U.S. threats: Daniel Ellsberg, in E. P. Thompson and Dan Smith, eds., *Protest and Survive* (New York: Monthly Review Press, 1981) i–ii.

Sayre (1930): John M. Swomley, "John Nevin Sayre: Part II," *Fellowship* 44:6 (June 1978) 8.

Barnet: *Giants,* p. 24.

World Military and Social Expenditures is available from World Priorities, Box 1003, Leesburg, VA 22075. These figures are from the 1979 edition, p. 23.

116 Paraplegic veteran: John Crown, quoted in Howard A. Rusk, M.D., *A World to Care For* (New York: Random House, 1972) 125–26. John Crown died a year later, of complications.

117 Woolman: *Journals,* p. 146.

Questionnaire: John E. Mack, "Psychosocial Effects of the Nuclear Arms Race," *Bulletin of the Atomic Scientists* 37:4 (Apr. 1981) 19.

118 Gandhi: *Harijan,* July 28, 1946.

118–19 Lieutenant Calley: quoted in Liane E. Norman, "The Spell of War," *The Center Magazine* 12 (Mar.–Apr. 1979) 74.

119 Grain-bag campaign: Alfred Hassler, "Sixty Years," *Fellowship* 41:8 (Dec. 1975) 12–13.

121 Figure 3: adapted from material prepared by Peter Frank, Curator, Germanic Material, Green Library, Stanford University, Stanford, Calif.

8 / Right Occupation

123 Peter Ognibene, "Vanishing Farmlands: Selling Out the Soil," *Saturday Review,* May 1980, p. 30.

123–24 Automobile assembler: now wildlife biologist John Mitchell, writing in "Bitter Harvest," *Audubon Magazine* 79:3 (May 1977) 55–56.

124 Ogilvy: from an advertising brochure for the *Progressive,* n.d.

124–25 High school enlistee: *San Francisco Chronicle,* January 30, 1980.

125 Dr. Samenow: *The National Observer,* July 11, 1977. See also Fromm, *Anatomy of Human Destructiveness,* pp. 278–82.

de Beauvoir: quoted in Charles Muscatine and Marlene Griffith, *First Person Singular* (New York: Knopf, 1973) 141.

Roszak, "Ethics, Ecstasy, and the Study of the New Religions," in Jacob Needleman and George Baker, eds., *Understanding the New Religions* (New York: Seabury Press, 1978) 61–62.

126 Frankl: *Man's Search for Meaning,* pp. 154, 122 (his italics).

Convalescent hospital experiment: *Family Practice News,* May 15, 1980.

127 E. F. Schumacher, "Alternatives in Technology," *Alternatives* 1 (1975) 10–11.

127–28 Camp experiment: M. Sherif, *In Common Predicament: Social Psychology of Intergroup Conflict and Cooperation* (Boston: Houghton Mifflin, 1966) 88–92.

128 Decline of farming life: Berry, *The Unsettling of America*, pp. 63, viii, 11; Ognibene, "Vanishing Farmlands."

129 Einstein friends: quotes from Ernst G. Strauss in the *Long Beach Independent Press-Telegram*, October 3–4, 1979.

132 Santa Clara conversion project: *Plowshare Press* 1:4 (Winter 1977). The direct quotes are from pp. 66 and 5 of that issue. For more recent information on the Lucas project, see ibid. 6:5 (Sept.–Oct. 1981).

134 Nelson Shields: *Christian Science Monitor*, March 1976 (exact date not ascertainable); see his *Guns Don't Die—People Do* (New York: Arbor, 1981) for further details.

Helen Caldicott, M.D., *Nuclear Madness: What You Can Do!* (Brookline, Mass.: Autumn Press, 1978) 105.

135 Gandhi: Easwaran, *Gandhi the Man*, p. 125.

135–36 "Strike in reverse": James McNeish, *Fire Under the Ashes: The Life of Danilo Dolci* (London: Hodden, 1965) 102–130.

136 Santa Rosa mothers: *Santa Rosa Press-Democrat*, November 13, 1977.

137 Gandhi and Gunther: Easwaran, *Gandhi the Man*, p. 106.

138 Roger Fisher: published in several places, among them as "To Gain a Peace in the Nuclear Age," in *Technology Review* 83:5 (Apr. 1981) 65, 69–70. This article is highly recommended and will be reprinted in my forthcoming collection, *Peace Now or Never*.

9 / LOVE FOR ALL

139 Hockey player: *Christian Science Monitor*, February 5, 1982.

"The greatest force": Fey, *Kirby Page*, p. 116.

140 George Fox: *Journals*, p. 330.

The Buddha: *Dhammapada*, chap. 26 (unpublished translation by Eknath Easwaran).

Gandhi: Easwaran, *Gandhi the Man*, p. 125.

141 Birmingham confrontation: Lynd, *Nonviolence in America*, pp. 525–26.

British police: Richard Gregg, *The Power of Nonviolence* (New York: Schocken, 1966) 28.

Martin Luther King, *Stride Toward Freedom*, p. 84.

143 Emerson: "Self Reliance," in Stephen E. Whicher, ed., *Selections from Ralph Waldo Emerson* (Boston: Houghton Mifflin, 1957) 160.

Rabbi Tamaret, "Non-Violence and the Passover," *Judaism* 17 (Spring 1968) 208.

144 Henry David Thoreau, *Walden and "Civil Disobedience"* (New York: Signet Classics, 1960) 237.

145–47 The Salt Satyāgraha: Louis Fisher, *Life of Mahatma Gandhi* (New York: Macmillan, 1962) 272–79.

148 British criminal justice reform: *Jericho* (newsletter of the National Moratorium on Prison Construction), no. 18 (Fall 1979) 6.

149 Atlanta episode: heard on the radio in that city.

150 Joan Bondurant, *The Conquest of Violence: The Ghandian Philosophy of Conflict,* 2d ed. (Berkeley: University of California Press, 1971) v.

Martin Luther King, *Stride Toward Freedom,* p. 198.

150–51 Ammon Hennacy: Lynd, *Nonviolence in America,* pp. 209–10.

152 Gandhi: Easwaran, *Gandhi the Man,* p. 114.

GI: David Parks, in Muscatine and Griffith, *First Person Singular,* p. 21.

Robert N. Bellah, "Cultural Vision and the Human Future," *Teachers College Record* 82:3 (Spring 1981) 497–506.

Erasmus: *The Complaint of Peace* (Chicago: Open Court, 1917) 56.

152–53 Storm Jameson, "The Twilight of Reason," in Philip Noel-Baker et al., *Challenge to Death* (London: Constable, 1934) 324–25 (her italics).

153 Orwell, *The Road to Wigan Pier* (New York: Harcourt Brace Jovanovich, 1958) 149.

Jawaharlal Nehru, *Toward Freedom—The Autobiography of Jawaharlal Nehru* (Boston: Beacon Press, 1958) 137.

154 Mumford on Emerson: *Christian Science Monitor,* November 29, 1974 (an interview about Mumford's *Interpretations and Forecasts*).

155 Gandhi: Easwaran, *Gandhi the Man,* p. 88.

FURTHER READING

The general effect of reading this book will not be to produce a reading jag. However, it seems useful to list some titles that can take the reader farther in various directions. The selection is brief and highly personal.

MEDIA AND OTHER ILLS

Bronfenbrenner, Urie. "The Origins of Alienation." *Scientific American* 231 (Aug. 1974) 53–61.

Brown, Richard Maxwell. *Strain of Violence: Historical Studies of American Violence and Vigilantism.* New York: Oxford University Press, 1975.

Mander, Jerry. *Four Arguments in Favor of the Elimination of Television.* New York: Morrow, 1978.

Somers, Anne R., M.D. "Violence, Television, and the Health of American Youth." *New England Journal of Medicine* 294:15 (Apr. 8, 1976) 811–17 (and Dr. Inglefinger's editorial in that issue).

Winn, Marie. *The Plug-In Drug: Television, Children, and the Family.* New York: Viking, 1977.

Yeager, Robert C. *Seasons of Shame: The New Violence in Sports.* New York: McGraw-Hill, 1979.

For up-to-date statistics on media, social, and international violence, consult:

Gerbner, G., and Gross, L. *Violence Profile.* Philadelphia: University of Pennsylvania, Annenberg School of Communications, 1967–on.

Sivard, Ruth Leger. *World Military and Social Expenditures.* Box 1003, Leesburg, Va. 22075; World Priorities. World Priorities also publishes *World Energy Survey.*

U.S. Department of Health, Education, and Welfare, National Center for Health Statistics. *Annual Summary for the United States, Final Mortality Statistics,* and other publications.

U.S. Department of Justice. *Sourcebook on Criminal Justice Statistics.* Albany, N.Y.: Criminal Justice Research Center.

FOOD FOR THOUGHT: GUIDES FOR UNDERSTANDING

Berry, Wendell. *The Unsettling of America: Culture and Agriculture.* San Francisco: Sierra Club, 1977.

Boulding, Kenneth E. *Stable Peace.* Austin: University of Texas Press, 1978.

Cousins, Norman. *Human Options.* New York: Norton, 1981.

_____. *In Place of Folly.* New York: Washington Square, 1962.

Easwaran, Eknath. *The Supreme Ambition.* Petaluma, Calif.: Nilgiri Press, 1982.

_____. *Dialogue with Death.* Petaluma, Calif.: Nilgiri Press, 1981.

Frankl, Viktor E. *Man's Search for Meaning.* New York: Pocket Books, 1963.

Gussow, Joan Dye. *The Feeding Web: Issues in Nutritional Ecology.* Palo Alto, Calif.: Bull, 1978.

Kropotkin, Peter. *Mutual Aid: A Factor in Evolution.* Boston: Porter Sargent, Extending Horizons, 1980.

_____. *Fields, Factories and Workshops Tomorrow.* New York: Harper & Row, 1974.

Lappé, Frances Moore, and Collins, Joseph. *Food First: Beyond The Myth of Scarcity.* New York: Ballantine, 1979.

Leakey, Richard, and Lewin, Roger. *Origins: What New Discoveries Reveal about the Emergence of Our Species and Its Possible Future.* New York: Dutton, 1977.

Montagu, Ashley. *The Nature of Human Aggression.* New York: Oxford University Press, 1976.

Schumacher, E. F. *Small Is Beautiful: Economics As If People Mattered.* New York: Harper & Row, 1973.

GANDHI AND COMPANY

The best selection of Gandhi's own sayings and writings is Krishna Kripalani, ed., *All Men Are Brothers,* reprint ed. (Chicago: World Without War, 1972). A larger and well-indexed version for those who wish to go further is R. K. Prabhu and U. R. Rao, *The Mind of Mahatma Gandhi,* rev. ed. (Ahmedabad: Navajivan, 1967). Garland Publishing Company, New York and London, is bringing out an American edition of the complete works of Gandhi with excellent editorship as part of its invaluable *Garland Library of War and Peace.* Reading the articles of Gandhi and his secretary Mahadev Desai as they appeared in *Harijan,* Gandhi's newspaper from the tumultuous days of the freedom struggle, gives a sense of the man and his work as nothing else can. Desai's diaries are almost as good for this, so far published in selected form by Navajivan Trust (first volume, 1953) but not in the West.

Of Gandhi's own books I recommend: *Satyāgraha in South Africa*

(Ahmedabad: Navajivan, 1950) and *An Autobiography, or the Story of My Experiments with Truth,* reprint ed. (Ahmedabad: Navajivan, 1959).

The people at Greenleaf Books, Weare, N.H., will send you what they consider the most important titles in stock by and about Gandhi for however much money you send them. The following might be considered the essential secondary works on Gandhi:

Bondurant, Joan. *The Conquest of Violence: The Gandhian Philosophy of Conflict.* 2d ed. Berkeley: University of California Press, 1971.

Easwaran, Eknath. *Gandhi the Man.* 2d ed. Petaluma, Calif.: Nilgiri Press, 1978. Best account of Gandhi's spiritual power.

Fischer, Louis. *Gandhi, His Life and Message for the World.* New York: Signet Books, 1954. The unabridged version is *The Life of Mahatma Gandhi* (New York: Collier Books, 1962).

Naess, Arne. *Gandhi and Group Conflict.* Oslo: Universitetsvorlaget, 1972. This book presents the best philosophical analysis of Gandhi's thought.

Shirer, William. *Gandhi: A Memoir.* New York: Simon & Schuster, 1979. This is one of the most sensitive accounts ever written of Gandhi in action, although the last chapter goes off the rails.

OTHER BOOKS ABOUT NONVIOLENCE AND ITS PRACTITIONERS

Ballou, Adin. *Christian Non-Resistance in all its Important Bearings, Illustrated and Defended.* Facsimile reprint ed. Englewood, N.J.: Jerome S. Ozer, 1972.

Brinton, Howard. *Friends for 300 Years: The History and Beliefs of the Society of Friends Since George Fox Started the Quaker Movement.* New York: Harper, 1952.

Brittain, Vera. *Rebel Passion: A Short History of Some Pioneer Peace Makers.* Nyack, N.Y.: Fellowship of Reconciliation, 1967.

Gregg, Richard. *The Power of Nonviolence.* Nyack, N.Y.: Fellowship of Reconciliation, 1959.

King, Martin Luther, Jr. *Stride Toward Freedom: The Montgomery Story.* New York: Perennial Library, 1967.

Sharp, Gene. *The Politics of Nonviolent Action.* Boston: Porter Sargent, 1973.

Stanford, Barbara. *Sixty Peace Heroes.* Kent, Ohio: Consortium on Peace Research, Education, and Development, Kent State University, forthcoming.

The following two anthologies, the first documentary, the second pictorial (and including an excellent bibliography), are extremely useful. (The reader should be aware, however, that both tend to limit nonviolence to the context of struggles against oppression and to define it as any technique that stops short of physical violence):

Cooney, Robert, and Michalowski, Helen. *The Power of the People, Active Nonviolence in the United States.* Culver City, Calif.: Peace Press, 1977.

Lynd, Staughton. *Nonviolence in America: A Documentary History.* New York: Bobbs-Merrill, 1966.

MEDITATION

This field is as personal as it is important. It would be misleading to present a survey, and I recommend only three books of whose effectiveness I have some personal experience:

Easwaran, Eknath. *Instructions in Meditation* (1972). Presents the basic instructions; also available in Spanish.

———. *Meditation* (1978). Presents the same instructions as *Instructions in Meditation* but with fuller explanatory—and inspirational—material.

———. *The Mantram Handbook* (1977).

All published by Nilgiri Press, Box 477, Petaluma, Calif. 94953. Tapes and records are also available from Nilgiri Press.

ACTION GUIDES

All that you wanted to know about organizations and resources for peace-producing and violence-reducing action will probably be listed in Martha Henderson, Ron Glass, and Diane Thomas-Glass, comps., *By Our Own Lives*, distributed by the Agape Foundation, 85 Carl Street, San Francisco, Calif. 94117. For gun control, however, which *By Our Own Lives* omits, see U.S. Conference of Mayors, *Organization for Handgun Control: A Citizen's Manual*, available from the National Council to Ban Handguns, 100 Maryland Avenue NE, Washington, D.C. 20002, and Pete Shields, *Guns Don't Die—People Do*, available at local bookstores or from Handgun Control, Inc. Kate Moody now has further suggestions on television: *Growing Up on Television* (New York: New York Times Books, 1980). A "Nuclear Arms Control Hotline" has just been set up by the Council for a Liveable World—(202) 543-0006—to give up-to-the-minute data on pending legislation on that issue.

INDEX

175

Films, 28
  on set near bomb test, 110
  violent, 18–19, 21, 23, 24, 27, 29
Fischer, Louis, 145, 146–147
Fisher, Roger, 138
"Flipper" (television program), 25
Florida, death penalty in, 69
Food supply
  animal, 128–129
  for China, 119–120
  and farmland loss, 128
  global, 14–15, 113
Football violence, 89, 90
Forster, E. M., 82
Fox, George, 73–74, 76, 140, 149
France
  Algeria and, 85
  history education in, 71
  nuclear weapons tests by, 112, 119
  refugees rescued in, 42
  Sandwich Islanders' resistance against, 84
Frankl, Viktor, 42, 62, 125–126
Freedom, isolating, 41–42
Freedom of conscience, Quakers and, 76
Freud, Sigmund, 102
Friends. See Quakers
Fröding, Gustaf, 72
Fromm, Erich, 60

Galbraith, John Kenneth, 78, 92
Games, 66, 89, 90–91. See also Sports
Games People Play (Berne), 9
Gandhi, Kasturba, 142
Gandhi, Mahatma K., 80, 81, 84–85, 118, 139, 142, 152, 153, 155
  anger conversion by, 98–100, 101, 102
  on bell curve, 37
  Bhave and, 94
  and history, 72, 80
  and human nature, 51
  and love, 80, 99–100, 101, 102, 135, 140, 143–144
  and Norwegian schoolteachers' strike, 82
  Plowshare Press and, 133
  and satyāgraha, 145–147, 149, 150
  and work, 123, 135, 137
Gandhi, Manilal, 146
Gang warfare films, 18–19, 23, 27
Garrison, William Lloyd, 78, 80
Gas shortage violence, 47, 116
Genesis, 31

Genetics, of behavior, 58
Gentle Tasaday (Nance), 65
Gerbner, George, 20, 25
Germany
  housing project in, 42
  nonviolence in language of, 139, 142
  resistance movements in, 85–86
  wives' demonstration in, 83
  working off offenses in, 148
  See also Gestapo
Gestapo
  and Norwegian schoolteachers' strike, 82
  refugees rescued from, 42
  and Rosenstrasse wives' demonstration, 83
  Szent-Györgyi and, 81
Gewaltfreiheit (German word), 142
Gewehrlosigkeit (German word), 139
Gilbert, William, 144
Global Education Associates, 87
God's Little Acre (Caldwell), 134–135
Gofman, John W., 110
Goodall, Jane, 55
Gould, Stephen, 58
Governments (general)
  censorship by, 28
  nonviolence and, 148–149
  war-causing, 115
Grass-roots organization, 136
Gravity, 143–144, 145, 152
Great Britain. See Britain
Greek balance of power, 111
Greek creation myth (Plato), 51–53, 57, 60, 63
Grotius, Hugo, 75
Gun control, 5, 134
Guns, 5–7, 20, 67, 108–109
Guns and Ammo (magazine), 5
Gunther, John, 137

Haldane, J. B. S., 40
Handguns, 5–7, 20
Happiness, 129
Harlow, Harry, 91
Harlow, Margaret, 91
Hayward, Susan, 110
Hazlitt, William, 61
Hellenic balance of power, 111
"Helter-Skelter" (Beatles), 21
Helter-Skelter (film), 21
Hennacy, Ammon, 150–151

Military values and perspectives, 87
Milk, Harvey, 45
Miller, Webb, 82, 146–147
Mindanao, Tasaday on, 65
Mische, Patricia, 88
Mitchell, Edgar, 113
Models, of human relationships, 10–16, 23, 44. *See also* Separateness; Unity
Modern Times (film), 123
Money, as work value, 123, 125
Monkeys
    brain stimulation of, 59
    facial expressions of, 59
    play-deprived, 91
Moorehead, Agnes, 110
Morocco, Algeria and, 85
Moscone, George, 37, 45
Mother Teresa of Calcutta, 40–41, 137
Mott, Lucretia, 80
Movies. *See* Films
Multicellular organism, evolution of, 62
Mumford, Lewis, 154
Murder. *See* Homicides
Murder mysteries, 18
Muskets, in New Zealand, 67
Muste, A. J., 80
Mutual Aid (Kropotkin), 43–44, 57
Mutual aid factor, 57, 139. *See also* Co-operation
My Lai massacre, 118, 119

Naidu, Sarojini, 146
Nance, John, 65
National Arbitration League, 79
National Center for Health Statistics, 38
National Council to Control Handguns, 134
NATO, 112
Naturalists, 55–57
Nature
    human, 51–69
    scientists observing, 70
Nausea, from films, 24
Nazis. *See* Gestapo
Nehru, Jawaharlal, 153
Netherlands, working off offenses in, 148
Nevada
    atomic bomb testing in, 110
    civil defense in, 109
Nevill, W. P., 89
New England Journal of Medicine, 28
New Jersey, television-avoiding experiment in, 26

News
    distortion in, 70–71
    violence in, 17, 18
Newspapers
    news distortion in, 70–71
    violence in, 18
Newton, Isaac, 143
New York City
    driving episode in, 115–116
    murder incidence in, 61
New Zealand, Maori of, 67
Nicaragua, John Nevin Sayre in, 80
Nixon, Richard M., 19
Nobel, Alfred B., 72
Nonviolence, 136, 139–155
    by blacks, 78, 80, 83, 141
    in colonial America, 73–74, 75–76, 77, 78
    in India, 76, 80–85 *passim*, 137, 141, 142, 145–147, 150, 153
    legitimation of, 87
    in nature, 55–56
    against Nazis, 82–83
    notable comparisons using, 80–86
    in primitive cultures, 65–66
    in Sicily, 135–136
    in South Africa, 83
    See also Cooperation; Gandhi, Mahatma K.; Love; Peace
North America
    new arrivals' violence in, 65
    radiation vs. combat fatalities in, 110
    See also Canada; United States
Northeastern University Center for Applied Social Research, 8
Norwegian schoolteachers' strike, 82, 83
Nuclear attack
    defense against, 108–109
    megadeaths from, 45
Nuclear war, students' thoughts of, 117
Nuclear weapons
    and deterrence, 106, 107, 112
    testing of, 110, 112, 119
Nuremberg housing project, 42

Oakland, California, gun killing in, 6
Obedience, vs. conscience, 118
Office work, 127
Ogilvy, David, 124
Ognibene, Peter, 123
Ohio
    gun ownership in, 6
    military academy planned in, 87

Also available from Island Press,
Star Route 1, Box 38, Covelo, California 95428

Tree Talk: The People and Politics of Timber, by Ray Raphael. Illustrations by Mark Livingston. $12.00
A probing analysis of modern forestry practices and philosophies. In a balanced and informed text, *Tree Talk* presents the views of loggers, environmentalists, timber industry executives, and forest farmers and goes beyond the politics of "production versus protection" to propose new ways to harvest trees and preserve forest habitats in a healthy economy and a thriving environment.

An Everyday History of Somewhere, by Ray Raphael. Illustrations by Mark Livingston. $8.00
This work of history and documentation embraces the life and work of ordinary people, from the Indians who inhabited the coastal forests of northern California to the loggers, tanbark strippers, and farmers who came after them. This loving look at history takes us in a full circle that leads to the everyday life of us all.

Pocket Flora of the Redwood Forest, by Dr. Rudolf W. Becking. Illustrations. $15.00
The most useful and comprehensive guidebook available for the plants of the world-famous redwood forest. Dr. Rudolf W. Becking, a noted botanist and Professor of Natural Resources, is also a gifted artist. The *Pocket Flora* includes detailed drawings, a complete key, and simple, accurate descriptions for 212 of the most common species of this unique plant community, as well as eight pages of color photographs. Plasticized cover for field use.

A Citizen's Guide to Timber Harvest Plans, by Marylee Bytheriver. Illustrations. $1.50
California state law permits any interested citizen to learn the details of proposed timber cutting on private or public lands. This report instructs citizens on their rights concerning timber harvesting, the procedures for influencing the details of proposed logging operations, and the specialized vocabulary surrounding the Timber Harvest Plan. A resource for action.

Wellspring: A Story from the Deep Country, by Barbara Dean. Illustrations. $6.00
The moving, first-person account of a contemporary woman's life at the edge of wilderness. Since 1971, Barbara Dean has lived in a handmade yurt on land she shares with fifteen friends. Their struggles, both hilarious and poignant, form the background for this inspiring story of personal growth and deep love for nature.

The Book of the Vision Quest: Personal Transformation in the Wilderness, by Steven Foster with Meredith E. Little. Photographs. $10.00
The inspiring record of modern people enacting an ancient, archetypal rite of passage. This book shares the wisdom and the seeking of many persons who have known the opportunity to face themselves, their fears, and their courage, and to live in harmony with nature through the experience of the traditional Vision Quest. Excerpts from participants' journals add an intimate dimension to this unique account of human challenge.

The Trail North, by Hawk Greenway. Illustrations. $7.50
The summer adventure of a young man who traveled the spine of coastal mountains from California to Washington with only his horse for a companion. The book he has

made from this journey reveals his coming of age as he studies, reflects, and greets the world that is awakening within and around him.

Building an Ark: Tools for the Preservation of Natural Diversity Through Land Protection, by Phillip M. Hoose. Illustrations. $12.00
The author is national protection planner for the Nature Conservancy, and this book presents a comprehensive plan that can be used to identify and protect what remains of each state's natural ecological diversity. Case studies augment this blueprint for conservation.

Headwaters: Tales of the Wilderness, by Ash, Russell, Doog, and Del Rio. Preface by Edward Abbey. Photographs and illustrations. $6.00
Four bridge-playing buddies tackle the wilderness—they go in separately, meet on top of a rock, and come out talking. These four are as different as the suits in their deck of cards, as ragged as a three-day beard, and as eager as sparks.

Perfection Perception, with the Brothers O. and Joe de Vivre. $5.00
Notes from a metaphysical journey through the mountains of Patagonia. The authors share their experiences and discoveries in using their powers of perception to change the world. Their thoughts are mystical at times, but their basis is firmly experiential and parallels the most theoretically advanced works in modern physics.

The Search for Goodbye-to-Rains, by Paul McHugh. $7.50
Steve Getane takes to the road in an American odyssey that is part fantasy and part real—a haphazard pursuit that includes Faulkner's Mississippi, the rarefied New Mexico air, and a motorcycle named Frank. "A rich, resonant novel of the interior world. Overtones of Whitman, Kerouac."—Robert Anton Wilson

No Substitute for Madness: A Teacher, His Kids & The Lessons of Real Life, by Ron Jones. Illustrations. $8.00
Seven magnificent glimpses of life as it is. Ron Jones is a teacher with the gift of translating human beauty into words and knowing where to find it in the first place. This collection of true experiences includes "The Acorn People," the moving story of a summer camp for handicapped kids, and "The Third Wave," a harrowing experiment in Nazi training in a high school class—both of which were adapted for television movies.

The Christmas Coat, by Ron Jones. Illustrations. $4.00
A contemporary fable of a mysterious Christmas gift and a father's search for the sender, which takes him to his wife, his son, and his memories of big band and ballroom days.

Please enclose $1.00 with each order for postage and handling.
California residents, add 6% sales tax.
A catalog of current and forthcoming titles is available free of charge.